MAKE A GREAT
WEDDING
SPEECH

Also by Philip Calvert

Successful Seminar Selling
The ultimate small business guide to boosting sales and profits through seminars and workshops

'This book is ideal for small business owners as it reveals one of the most profitable ways of promoting your company – Seminar Selling.' – Digby Jones, Director-General, Confederation of British Industry

'The ideas and tips in this book are invaluable and will add not only confidence to any speaker, but additional income streams to any business.' – Frank Furness, International Motivational Speaker

howtobooks

For full details, please send for a free copy of the latest catalogue to:

How To Books
3 Newtec Place, Magdalen Road
Oxford OX4 1RE, United Kingdom
info@howtobooks.co.uk
www.howtobooks.co.uk

MAKE A GREAT
WEDDING
SPEECH

PHILIP CALVERT

howto**books**

Every effort has been made to identify and acknowledge the sources of the material quoted throughout this book. The author and publishers apologise for any errors or omissions, and would be grateful to be notified of any corrections that should appear in any reprint or new edition.

Published by How To Books Ltd
3 Newtec Place, Magdalen Road
Oxford, OX4 1RE, United Kingdom
Tel: (01865) 793806. Fax: (01865) 248780
email: info@howtobooks.co.uk
www.howtobooks.co.uk

British Library Cataloguing in Publication Data
A catalogue record for this book is available from the British Library

Edited by Francesca Mitchell
Cover design by Baseline Arts Ltd, Oxford
Cover photos © Peter Jones www.pjweddings.com
Produced for How To Books by Deer Park Productions, Tavistock
Typeset by TW Typesetting, Plymouth, Devon
Printed and bound by Cromwell Press, Trowbridge, Wiltshire

To Sarah

This all started at our wedding –
'the third Calvert wedding of the year'.
What a wonderful day that was. I'll never forget it.

Contents

Preface

Some years ago I used to be a photographer. I took snaps of everything and anything, but particularly enjoyed taking pictures at weddings and rock concerts. Very often a roll of film had a picture of a beautiful smiling bride in white at one end and Lemmy from Motörhead at the other. The trick was to separate the two before handing over the proofs.

It was my father, Brian, who first introduced me to the art. In hindsight, I'm surprised at my later interest in photography given how long it would take him to take a picture. He was never really one for scenic views but took many family close-ups:

'Hold it there . . . smile everyone . . . move to the side a bit, wait . . . good, say 'cheese'. Hold on while I get you in focus . . . good – keep still, keep smiling. Wait for it . . .'

Click!

We always got there in the end and whilst the results were good, well framed and (let's face it) *in focus* family pictures, my brothers, mother and I often looked just a little stilted and wooden with beaming, but stiff smiles.

'Beaming, but stiff' is a phrase I could also use to describe the guests during the speeches at many of the weddings I photographed, but it is not a phrase I could use to describe the attendees at the rock concert I photographed later the same day. 'Beaming' maybe, but definitely not 'stiff'.

The difference of course lies in the degree to which an audience or guests are enthused, excited or moved by the 'main act' – whether it be the bride's father, groom or best man, or indeed our friends in Motörhead.

And today, it's not just the men who are making the speeches. Brides' mothers are springing to their feet at weddings everywhere to 'say a few words', not to mention grooms' mothers and the occasional auntie.

Not all that long ago, the wedding ceremony and the festivities afterwards were carefully choreographed with every step, turn and mouthful planned, prepared and re-hearsed with meticulous detail. But today's more relaxed society often brings a healthy dose of informality to proceedings affecting everything from how the bride arrives at the church (on Harley-Davidson motorcycles, steam rollers, fire engines and so on), to the music (how many times have you heard Bryan Adams's 'Everything I do I do it For You'?) and the speeches (often courtesy of material from a Bob Monkhouse book or one of the many websites now offering speech advice).

Informality is one thing, poor taste another. Bob Monkhouse was a master of the mother-in-law joke, but of course he could get away with it – not forgetting the small but important fact that he was a professional comedian. I've been to a lot of weddings in my time, but not one of the grooms or best men were 'funny for a living'. Most were either accountants, IT professionals, plumbers, solicitors, engineers, sales people, conference organisers or estate agents, but for some reason many felt that their wedding speech was the time to announce their new career as the next Bob Hope, Rowan Atkinson or Bob Monkhouse himself.

The difference is that Bob knew how to tell a mother-in-law joke 'properly'. After all, he probably wrote the joke in the first place and then practised it two hundred times before it saw the light of day. Professional comedians and speakers do that. Even if they have great script writers like Barry Cryer, they still practise, practise and practise until they can do it perfectly. To achieve that extra bit of star quality, they have honed their craft in smoke-filled nightclubs up and down the country.

So it's unfortunate that a great many men feel that very little rehearsal and resorting to the internet or Bob's fine work will result in a superb wedding speech. And even if for some reason they feel that telling a mother-in-law joke is a good idea as part of their wedding speech, why is it that they think they can get away with using someone else's material?

I'll be the first to admit that we don't all necessarily have the time to rehearse our speech before the big day and it's easy to see how tempting pre-prepared material can be. But even with the slightly more informal approach to many of today's weddings, our guests are expecting a good perform-ance – *from you* – the groom, best man or bride's father, or whoever – not Bob Monkhouse.

If you have ever been fortunate enough to have seen Rowan Atkinson's one man show or are the proud owner of his *Live in Belfast* recording from 1980, you will doubtless have split your sides with laughter at his wedding sketch. This remarkable send-up of the speeches made by the best man and the father of the bride is funny on a number of levels – not least because to a greater or lesser extent they are a fantastic parody of speeches heard at virtually every wedding.

The problem comes when the best man and the father of the bride decide that Rowan's material will form the basis of their own speeches. And not just 'form the basis' either. On more than one occasion I have witnessed well-meaning but foolhardy men start and end their comedy careers at either their best friend's or daughter's wedding. They didn't just use a couple of well-chosen lines from the recording, but 'performed' the entire sketch to their beaming (but not quite sure where to look) guests. You may even have seen this appalling spectacle with your own eyes and, as a friend who had to sit through one such performance once told me – 'It was so cringingly awful, I winced with embarrassment.'

I guess that most of us would probably be a little disappointed if our wedding guests described our speech as 'cringingly awful' or 'embarrassing', but all too often that is exactly how it comes across. Of course, no one's going to tell you – are they?!

So this book has been written for people who might just be tempted to resort to using other people's material for their wedding speech, whether it be from a book of one-liners or one of the many wedding websites. There's even one website which generates an instant speech based on the answers you give to a few simple online questions!

In my view, there is nothing to beat a wedding speech which has been put together by you and delivered with self-assurance, sincerity, joy, passion and love. We will reveal how to prepare yourself and your own material and in ways which suit your individual character and style.

You will also discover the golden rules of making a great wedding speech; how to cope with nerves, how to make a superb impact, how to rehearse when time is short and how to achieve that vital extra ingredient – star quality.

It's also important to remember that no two people are the same, so I've included special tips for people who are either very shy, nervous or even overconfident. And, if you have never spoken in public before, the tips included throughout the book will work for you too.

The book is *not* intended as a formal guide to wedding etiquette, procedures, planning or where to seat long lost aunties, alcoholic uncles or divorced parents who have remarried. It's about how to make a memorable wedding speech that you will enjoy giving and which the guests will enjoy hearing.

I also make no apologies for trying to bring the whole business of wedding speeches kicking and screaming right up to date. Today's more informal society permeates even the relative formality of a wedding and in particular the wedding reception, resulting in things being said and done at such occasions that would have been out of the question in the past. So I hope you will enjoy some of the stories and anecdotes from wedding speeches that I have collected.

Bringing the business of wedding speeches right up to date must also include gay marriages and partnerships. And whilst the world's gay community strives for same sex marriage to be more formally recognised, gay and lesbian couples will want to celebrate their union. Accordingly, the advice in this book is for everyone.

Thank you to all the grooms, best men, brides' fathers, brides and everyone who has contributed to this book – for either the right or the wrong reasons!

Philip Calvert, 2005

Acknowledgements

For their superb contributions, I would like to thank:

Tony and Freda Goodwill
Jeff Kay
David Calvert
John Calvert
Dan and Claire Wood
Simon and Jenny Hallett
Marie Mosely
Andy Gough
Maurice Watts
Simon Phillips
Jacqui Smith
Dr Andy Pardoe
Emma Hollingworth
Andrew Wilcox for his mind map expertise

My father Brian for his 'introduction to photography',
and my mum for the coaching on the stairs.

And all the others who wanted to remain anonymous.
You know who you are and you know why you want to
remain anonymous!

Part One
Planning Your Speech

When You Realise You Have to Make a Speech

'Will you marry me?'

These four little words fire the starting gun (hopefully) for what promises to be a roller coaster ride of emotions, planning and saving which will culminate in a wedding to remember for years to come.

FAST FACTS

You will no doubt have noticed that the cost of the big day is proving somewhat higher than you were expecting. But hey, what's £25,500 between friends? A survey by Cahoot, the internet bank, reveals that's what the average wedding costs today and it works out at £61.10 per minute.

According to the UK Office of National Statistics' *Marriage, Divorce and Adoption Report 2001*, women now marry on average at the age of 27 compared with the average age of 25 during the 1990s. Men now marry at 30 on average, compared with 26 just a few years ago.

It has been suggested that one of the reasons the cost of getting hitched is increasing is because at a more mature age men and women are more financially independent than when they were younger, and are thus able to splash out more on the exact wedding they want – whether it's on an exotic beach in the Caribbean, in a helicopter over New Zealand or at another romantic dream location. What's really important is that the wedding day is remembered for a long time to come. And quite right too.

I would hate to be cynical and suggest that the more you pay for your wedding, the more likely it is to be remembered, but all too often that can actually be the truth of the matter. On the other hand, it is entirely possible to have a truly memorable wedding for a very modest sum. Either way, many weddings are remembered for the wrong reason; a reason which hasn't cost a penny – the speeches.

FAIL TO PLAN – PLAN TO FAIL

There's a very simple reason why the speeches are remembered for the wrong reason and that's because they receive such scant attention and planning. This is a real shame, because the speeches can make a huge difference to the enjoyment of the day for everyone and greatly enhance your memories. By 'planning' I don't mean who proposes a toast to whom and when (we'll cover that in the next chapter). By 'planning' I mean:

◆ the detail of your speech

◆ how you gather material

◆ how you order it

◆ how you rehearse it

- how you prepare yourself

- how you deliver it with impact, self-assurance, style, flair, passion, joy and sincerity.

There comes a point during the planning of the wedding arrangements when you realise you are going to have to make a speech. To some people it comes quite early on, particularly if they have some experience of speaking in public. To others, the mind blocks it out until the last few weeks (or hours) before the big day and then it dawns on them that they will soon be called upon by the Toastmaster. It feels like being hit by a train.

For most people, speaking in public would not be their first choice of hobby or extra curricular activity. Depending on which piece of research you read, speaking in public ranks higher than bungee jumping or death on the 'things we most fear' charts. And it's worse when you have to do it in front of your closest friends and relatives. Even sales people find it easier to do a presentation to a group of two hundred strangers, business prospects or clients than to just ten of their work colleagues.

WHAT IS IT ABOUT MAKING A SPEECH THAT CAUSES US TO BECOME SO FEARFUL?

In my own experience I have found that in today's society we tend to make assumptions about what other people are expecting from us, whether in a social situation or at work. In a work environment there certainly are expectations of us, but at least they are known and expressed in the form of written formal objectives. If we don't come up to the standards set, we could be disciplined or even sacked. When we have to put on a talk as part of our work we also make assumptions about the audience's expectations of our presentation skills, but invariably these assumptions are incorrect. The problem is that during presentations *most speakers make a guess as to the expectations of their audience and focus on themselves rather than providing value to the listener.*

With the focus on ourselves rather than the listener, we are actually making the presentation task ahead more stressful than it need be. The reason we focus on ourselves is because we have not taken steps to find out the audience's expectations in terms of content, our level of expertise and delivery. As we don't know our audience's expectations we subconsciously assume they are expecting more than we have the competence to provide. In short, if we took more trouble to focus on the audience rather than ourselves, we would find it much less stressful.

The same is true when making a wedding speech. We put unnecessary stress on ourselves at a very early stage by subconsciously imagining the expectations of the guests. And if we imagine that making a wedding speech will be stressful and that the guests won't enjoy it, you can guess what happens.

QUICK TIP

In any presentation or wedding speech, don't fret over the detail of what you intend to say. Concentrate on speaking with sincerity, passion and conviction and you will find that your speech flows much more smoothly.

In fact, unless you make a complete fool of yourself by falling over drunk, most audiences are extremely tolerant of nerves and the occasional mistake. It is your content, sincerity and expertise that they are interested in, not your delivery. Your delivery can be worked on to enhance your message and make it more memorable.

The truth is that the guests know that making any speech is hard work and as a consequence they are not looking to lynch you if you foul up! Honest, they're not! And here's another thing – they are *not* expecting you to tell jokes like a seasoned pro, or to have the verbal lucidity, eloquence and articulacy of a newsreader, president or political leader at their annual conference. The guests at a wedding actually want you to enjoy yourself and to hear a few well chosen words of affection. If you can make it entertaining along the way, then all the better and in Part Two of this book you will discover a number of helpful tips.

IT'S A CONTROL THING

Another reason why making a wedding speech can terrify people – to the extent that it can potentially spoil the whole day for them – is because they feel that for the few minutes they are on their feet at the reception they have no *control* over the guests. For example will the guests enjoy the speech? Will they heckle? Will they nod off?

In fact, most of us find that *being in control* or being responsible for the guests' enjoyment is quite stressful. Having organised the day, we want and expect it to go well and this means everything *going to our plan*. We expect the weather to be fine, the flowers to look pretty, the cars to arrive on time, the dress to fit, the cake not to be soggy in the centre, the photos to come out, the vicar or registrar to be sober and so on, because *we planned it that way*. And so we also expect the guests to turn up, to behave, to smile and to enjoy themselves!

As we have planned everything so carefully, of course there will be no problems. But because the speech is such an unknown entity we rightly or wrongly feel that we have little control over the enjoyment of the guests during those few minutes when we are speaking, and this creates stress – albeit without us realising it.

QUICK TIP

My advice is not to concern yourself or worry about how guests will respond to your speech. At every wedding I have ever attended, the guests have not been out to cause trouble or to formally appraise the speakers afterwards.

Your job is not on the line if your speech isn't great – unless perhaps you've married the boss's daughter. However, one of the reasons people are still fearful is because they are facing the unknown when it comes to the speeches. Why unknown? Because they haven't given anything like enough thought to:

◆ the planning and structure of the speech

◆ the sentiments they want to communicate

◆ how they would like to be perceived by the guests

◆ what they want them to remember about their speech.

SUMMARY

Remember: 'If you fail to plan, you're planning to fail.' When you consider the amount of energy that goes into every other aspect of the wedding, wouldn't it be a good idea to take out some of the unknown by putting some effort into the speeches and planning them properly?

Over the following chapters we will show you how to plan and prepare a fantastic wedding speech and how to deliver it so that the wedding day will be remembered for years to come.

Who Says What and When

After the formality of the wedding ceremony where everything that is said or done has been carefully scripted and choreographed according to tradition and to the letter, the toasts and speeches come as a welcome respite for everyone – particularly when accompanied by a couple of glasses of bubbly.

Having got the 'official' ceremonial bits out of the way, it almost comes as a relief that people can now relax, chat, laugh and really start to enjoy themselves, with the guests eager to hear what the groom, best man and father of the bride have to say for themselves – if anything.

GREAT EXPECTATIONS

It is certainly *not* compulsory for speeches and toasts to be made but more of a traditional courtesy where acknowledgements are made to various parties. But today, there is always a frisson of expectation as the moment comes for the leading players to say their piece. The expectations of the guests are many and varied, with some anticipating traditional 'thank yous', acknowledgements and general grovelling, whilst others are preparing to wallow in a good hour of pledges of unadulterated love, affection, commitment, faithfulness, loyalty and utter devotion. Others are looking forward to world class entertainment of the highest calibre – and lots of it.

Unfortunately, many will be disappointed. Even at some of the grandest weddings, the content of the speeches can be a tad light on the ground, with often the vicar or registrar and the caterers getting more of a mention than the bride. Not uncommon are some of the following:

I just wanted to say thanks to you all for coming – particularly Uncle Graham and his new girlfriend Nicolette who have both come all the way from Paris. Help yourself to another drink. Thanks again for coming.

I think you will all agree that the bridesmaids look lovely – and so do the mums. And Cheryl – my lovely new wife – you've scrubbed up nicely too.

Er, I'm pretty crap at this, so am not going to say much. Thanks to everyone for coming. Hope you have a good time. Er, the bar's open – cheers.

My wife and I *(pause for laughter)* are both well pleased that you have all been able to turn up this afternoon – particularly as the footie is starting in a few minutes. Ha ha ha. We're now going to cut the cake.

THE BEAUTIFUL BRIDE VS THE BEAUTIFUL GAME

It never ceases to amaze me how often football and rugby are mentioned in wedding speeches. I have witnessed grooms and best men give pass-by-pass reports on 'last

Saturday's game' which would not have been out of place on *Match of the Day*. It's when the hotel staff are asked to find a small portable television that you start to worry about whether the marriage will still be going strong by the following weekend.

The casual observer would be forgiven for thinking that this unexpected addition to the proceedings was a humorous last minute brainwave, fuelled by champagne and the good humour of the day – and undertaken with the full authority of the bride. The fact that an impressive 51 inch widescreen rear-projection system is ceremoniously wheeled into the room like the Holy Grail suggests that this was planned in meticulous detail some five weeks earlier.

As the bride, her mother and their female entourage smile gamely, a raucous cheer erupts from the men in the room. Whilst he was fully implicated in the plot, the groom goes through the motions of protesting, but to no avail. The plug is pushed into the wall and the giant set is switched on, just as the referee blows his whistle for the start of the game. The bride of course blames the best man, and sharp looks are exchanged across the table. Little does she know that the real perpetrator of the plot will be sitting next to her on the plane to the Maldives in just a few hours from now.

WHAT TO DO AND SAY

Assuming that your wedding reception does not include the Merseyside Derby, what should you be doing and saying? We go into more detail as this book progresses, but here are some of the key things for each of the main speakers to remember.

THE FATHER OF THE BRIDE

Tradition has it that the bride's father kicks off (excuse the pun) proceedings, though very often the best man will say a few short words first by acting as MC. Many larger, grander weddings will employ the services of a 'proper' professional master of ceremonies or toastmaster, and this can be an extremely useful service for those who are not completely comfortable or familiar with the order of play.

Very often, the hotel or venue for the wedding reception will provide a toastmaster as part of the package. Apart from adding an extra air of grandeur to the occasion, such a service is invaluable, as he or she will be an expert on wedding protocol and procedures, and will help to ensure the smooth running of the day. You should not underestimate how important this is, as all too often, wedding receptions are allowed to drag on a bit, with guests wondering what is going to happen next, and when. I have been to many weddings where this has happened and it has the effect of upsetting the forward momentum of the event. It is best to keep things moving at a reasonable but relaxed pace, and this is best done by having a professional who is experienced in such matters. What's more, if the reception is allowed to proceed too slowly, this does add to the nervousness of the key speakers.

QUICK TIP

Regardless of whoever takes on the role of toastmaster or MC, speakers (whether at a wedding, conference or business event) should always be introduced by someone else.

The father of the bride is one of the 'big players' at the wedding, and should be billed as such, and by introducing him, his status is elevated to the right position for his speech. If the best man does not know the bride's father very well, they should get together beforehand to exchange notes. Alternatively, dad should provide a few notes or even write his own introduction for the best man to read. Although the point of doing a preamble is to 'tee up' the speech and the speaker, there is no reason why it shouldn't be humorous – perhaps something along the lines of an introduction I once heard:

> Our first speaker this afternoon, is of course Caroline's father – the man who made all of this possible. If you know Brian, you will of course know that despite having five lovely daughters, he claims to have led a very sheltered life – railway shelters, bus shelters . . .

And so on.

I once heard the late, great radio DJ Kenny Everett using the same 'sheltered life' line, but despite my concerns about repeating comedians' material, this worked well because of its brevity. The introduction should not be a speech in its own right – just what it says on the tin – and should last no longer than 30 seconds.

KEY FEATURES OF THE FATHER OF THE BRIDE'S SPEECH

The speech from the bride's father is generally considered to be the most measured of the three, and whilst it is occasionally seen as the 'warm up act' or scene setter, it is often the most heartfelt. Most of the speech will be concerned with reminiscences of his daughter, her childhood, her early teenage years and so on. It will also include some or all of the following:

- An official welcome to all the guests on behalf of his family.

- A thank you to everyone who has been involved with the organisation and (very often these days) the funding of the wedding.

- Welcoming of the groom to the family. This will include some initial observations of both his finer characteristics and some more humorous remarks.

- Welcome of the groom's family and how much he is looking forward to getting to know them.

- Comments and tributes to his own spouse.

- Special mention of any very close members of the family who are unable to attend or are indisposed (see best man below).

Finally, the bride's father will round off with his toast to the health (and increasingly the wealth) and happiness of the bride and groom.

THE GROOM

After the bride's father, the groom is next 'up to the ockey'. Again, it is a good idea for the best man to act as MC and to provide a short introduction. After all, the groom is one of the main players on the day, so a good lead in will create a strong sense of anticipation for the guests. Indeed, if the two introductions are particularly good, it will also enhance the guests' anticipation for the best man's speech later on.

The groom generally has the most to think about and do during his speech, poor lamb. And whilst he is making the speech, he is giving it on behalf of both himself *and* his wife. It is for this reason that we increasingly hear speeches from the bride as well, reflecting modern times where both the man and woman are the main breadwinners. It is only tradition that has decreed that just the groom should give the speech on behalf of the happy couple, so there is no reason at all why the bride should not make her own speech.

Woe betide the groom who does not mention his wife during his speech, and concentrates too much on his own friends, his work colleagues, football and his family – don't think it doesn't happen. I have seen brides give their new husband a hard dig in the ribs with their elbow when he failed to say *anything at all* about her! On the two occasions I saw this happen, both the grooms concerned were trying to do their speeches without notes, and in their effort to remember to thank everyone, completely forgot the person they had just married. You can imagine how this went down with the bride's parents.

KEY FEATURES OF THE GROOM'S SPEECH

In addition to dedicating a large proportion of the speech to his beautiful wife, here are some of the other things that the groom needs to remember:

- Thank you to the bride's father for his kind words, blessings and (where appropriate) his enormous generosity in paying for the wedding.

- Thank you to anyone else (perhaps his own family) for their financial contribution.

- Thank you to his own parents for, well, bringing him up to be an upstanding citizen.

- Thank you to everyone for accepting their invitation to the wedding and for their kind gifts.

- Thank you to his best man.

- Thank you to any ushers and other key helpers.

- A special toast on behalf of the bride and groom to the bridesmaids and pageboys.

QUICK TIP

As well as thanking them publicly, the pageboys and bridesmaids will often be presented with gifts, and the mothers may be given bouquets of flowers. This part of the speech when giant bouquets magically appear out of thin air always goes down well with the guests, but it can be a little predictable and samey from wedding to wedding.

I once attended a wedding where the groom didn't give any flowers, but gave each of the two sets of parents a weekend break at a country hotel (separately I might add). I have also seen a groom give each of the mums a voucher for treatments at a health spa. The more creative your gift, the more interesting it will be for the guests, and doubtless, what you do will be guided by your budget. Weddings are expensive enough as it is, without giving away holidays to all and sundry!

It is also increasingly common to thank either the registrar or church minister who conducted the marriage ceremony, and depending on how busy they are, many will be delighted to attend the reception as well – particularly if you are well known to them.

THE BEST MAN

> Apparently I'm supposed to tell a few jokes, but other than the bride's dress I can't think of any.
>
> Anon

It is important to remember that you are, in fact, the groom's *best* man, which technically means supporting him through-out the day. So it's odd how tradition has determined that humiliating him in your speech is in order!

The best man has the privilege of being the main act during the wedding speeches (though he is increasingly being upstaged by the bride), and whilst he will ideally be witty and entertaining, he also has one or two formal duties to perform. As best man you will have general organising to do on the day, for example, keeping people informed about timings, seating arrangements or maybe activities later in the evening. If there is not a toastmaster or master of ceremonies, the best man may well assume that role too.

KEY FEATURES OF THE BEST MAN'S SPEECH

Here are some of the things the best man will need to remember:

- Thank you to the groom (and the bride) for any kind remarks that were made to himself.

- Thank you to the bridesmaids and pageboys.

- Reading out any last minute cards and telegrams (more on this later).

- Propose a toast to the bride and groom. Make sure you give it everything you've got!

SUMMARY

Despite the relative informality of modern life, which increasingly pervades today's weddings, the order and content of the three main speeches remains firmly set in stone. Ideally, you should try to ensure that someone is responsible for making this happen and that each of the main speakers is introduced properly.

A professional master of ceremonies or toastmaster is preferable, but if not, a member of the hotel staff (if you are using one) will be familiar with the correct protocol and procedures. The speeches should be 'teed up' correctly, rather than letting everyone 'drift' as though no one is quite sure what to do next. If the speakers are introduced properly, this also has the effect of getting them 'on their marks' and ready for the gun to be fired.

3

The Golden Rules: What Makes a Memorable Speech

Perhaps it's their humour, charisma, personality, style, knowledge, expertise, entertainment value, sex appeal, personal magnetism, charm, celebrity or something else? It's a very personal thing, so just imagine how difficult it is to give a speech which appeals to *everyone* in the room – and all at the same time.

This is worth bearing in mind when you think about a typical guest list at a wedding these days. For starters, the age range will be extremely broad, with everyone from work colleagues to children, and teenagers to grandparents being present. Throw in a diverse range of friends from a variety of different backgrounds and cultures and you have an audience most unlike that at any other speaking situation.

Other than their knowledge of the happy couple and perhaps a few blood ties, they will have very little in common, thus making the speech even more challenging.

It's a fair bet that being passionate about their subject is also high up the list of things that attract us to a speaker or personality. Passion in a speech comes of a magical mixture of expertise, sincerity and charisma which results in everyone in the audience being inspired, motivated and hanging on to every word they hear. Whilst a wedding reception would not normally be regarded as the right time and place for a motivational speech, the guests do want to see sincerity, earnestness, charm, personality and *passion* – it is a wedding after all. They also want to be entertained.

Let's look at just some of the characteristics of good speakers and relate them to wedding speeches. Each one will be expanded upon later in this book, but it's important to get some key points under our belt straight away.

JUST DO IT!

Nerves are a problem for most people making a wedding speech, and some speakers don't actually start to enjoy the day until the speech is out of the way! The now famous advertisement for Nike captures the essence behind making a great wedding speech. The vast majority of people who have to 'perform' at the reception have never spoken in front of a group of people before, either at work or socially, so the thought of having to make a wedding speech has the potential to paralyse them with fear on what is supposed to be, for grooms at least, the happiest day of their life.

It sounds harsh, but frankly the only real way to get over this is to just bite your lip and get on with it. Even seasoned, regular business speakers get nervous before a talk, but at some stage they realise they've just got to get on with it.

QUICK TIP

The first 30 seconds will set the tone for the rest of the speech. Far better to take a deep breath, smile broadly and be determined to enjoy yourself. Think of the beautiful bride; this is her day, so don't let her down and just give it your all. You have nothing to lose!

USING NOTES

Whilst I don't fundamentally object to the use of notes or scripts (which we will cover later in this book), I have no doubt in my mind that the very best wedding speeches are given without any notes or cues at all.

Eye contact is vital in any form of human communication and the less there is of it, the less we tend to trust and engage with the person talking to us. I have seen countless wedding speeches where the groom, best man or father of the bride makes a point, stops, looks down, pauses, reads his notes, looks up, makes another point, stops, looks down again, pauses, reads notes, looks up, makes a point and so on. There is nothing that interrupts the flow of good communication like stopping to look down to find out what to say next, and straight away the audience feels that there is little or no sincerity in the message. The message *may well* be sincere and heartfelt, but it won't come across that way.

This one point alone will make a substantial difference to the quality of your speech, because you are forced to speak *how you feel*. In other words, your message will come straight from your heart. I'm not advocating that you don't prepare what you are going to say – this is absolutely vital. Even the most apparently 'off the cuff' speeches have been practised over and over again, and the more you practise, the better your speech will be.

Finally, by not using notes you will be seen as being different from the majority of other speakers and so your speech will be even more memorable.

BE CREATIVE AND DIFFERENT

Let's face it, if you think back over the weddings you have attended, most of the speeches are extremely similar in style, substance and delivery. And whilst a certain amount of formality is important it is entirely acceptable to be creative and help the guests to actually enjoy themselves.

Better though that you don't go as far as setting up a laptop and projector and treating the guests to a 45-minute powerpoint presentation complete with bullet points, clip art and animations. My next door neighbour was privileged to witness such a spectacle and told me that whilst there was initial novelty value, it soon wore off! Creativity is one thing, but do remember that this is a wedding, not an audition or a presentation to the board.

I have two younger brothers, David and John who are twins. Once at a wedding we all attended together, they shared the role of the best man and put on an excellent double act which gave an extra dimension to the traditional best man's speech. In short, the most memorable wedding speeches are those where the speaker has put in some effort *to make it memorable*. But don't overdo it. The idea is to be just a little inventive and original, not crazy and off the wall.

COMMUNICATE WITH THE GUESTS

We have already mentioned the importance of good eye contact with the guests to 'oil the wheels of communication'. Another way to help you communicate with them and to make your speech memorable is to interact with them, both verbally and physically.

QUICK TIP

Conducting your speech like a conversation also helps people to feel that you are not 'lecturing' them and also adds more life and animation to your talk. It will also help people to feel more a part of the occasion – particularly guests who are not members of the family.

There are no rules which say that those making the speech have to stand rooted to the spot. Why not move around a bit? Go up to a few people you know well and bring them into what you are saying. For example, if you are the best man and are telling a story which involves someone who also happens to be a guest, go up to them, put your hand on their shoulder and ask them to relate part of the story themselves. They won't thank you for it, but it makes for more entertainment for the other guests.

An old speaker trick to help oil the wheels of communication at seminars, conferences and meetings is to aim to meet and greet as many of the audience as possible before their talk begins. A key part of any 'speaking engagement' is to connect with people as this makes it much easier for you to get your message across, understood and remembered.

QUICK TIP

Experienced speakers will try hard to meet as many of the audience as possible – perhaps as they file into the seminar room, conference hall or wedding reception. The idea is to make a connection with people before you even get on your feet so that they (the audience) and you feel as though you already know each other and that you are not talking to a group of complete strangers. All it takes is a smile and a handshake and if possible a brief exchange of pleasantries.

At a wedding, the opportunity to meet people, communicate and exchange pleasantries is of course handed to you on a plate. What with all the hugging and kissing that goes on the wheels of communication are well and truly oiled right from the start.

MENTION GUESTS BY NAME

A really great tip for making your speech memorable is to mention as many of the guests as possible by name. If you have a couple of hundred people at your reception that could mean your speech going on well into the night, so in many situations this will clearly be impractical. But the more of your guests that you can get into your speech the better – even if it is just a list of people that you are thanking for a kindness at some stage over the years or in the planning (or paying) for the wedding. They *will* thank you for it and it will show you are not just thinking about yourself, but also care about your guests. Caring for the comfort and enjoyment of your audience is one of the most important points to remember in any public speaking situation, whether at work or at a wedding.

USING HUMOUR

Humour is said to be a universal communication tool, but it is surprising how little we consciously use it to get our message across, whatever the situation.

The wedding reception is the main opportunity to celebrate the marriage, but all too often they are very stiff, serious and stilted affairs. Quite often this is because everyone has got so wrapped up in all the organisation of the event that people forget that they should be enjoying themselves!

This comes over all too readily in the speeches, and whilst sincerity is important, the sentiments being expressed very often come across far too seriously. Brides' fathers tend to be most guilty of this and end up looking like a politician making a speech after having just lost their seat in an election. Of course, making a speech to your friends and relatives at your daughter's wedding is quite a big deal for any father, but your guests would prefer that your talk conveys happiness. This is, after all, a wedding speech – not a eulogy for a work colleague.

Humour, intentional or otherwise, is a big crowd pleaser at weddings. Whilst it is primarily for the benefit of the guests, it will often help you to feel more comfortable standing in front of everyone – particularly if you get some hearty laughs, which more often than not you will. Very often, the laughs will come at unexpected moments, which although have the potential to put you off your stride, are very welcome. Just occasionally, you will be one of those lucky people who find the guests rolling around in hysterics at just about everything and anything you say. It's a thrilling moment and one which subconsciously starts you thinking about a career in public speaking (believe me some guests will suggest this afterwards), but more importantly, results in a memorable wedding for everyone.

Unless you are a comedian, it is unlikely that you can plan for this to happen. Unfortunately, the dynamics of a wedding reception can conspire to create an audience that even seasoned professional speakers would rather avoid. It would certainly not be my audience of choice, but on the day it's the only one you've got. Occasionally, the heady cocktail of family politics, dodgy friends and champagne can work very much in your favour resulting in a truly great wedding speech. My advice is to just enjoy it while you can!

How to decide what sort of humour to use

We mentioned in the Preface that the late Bob Monkhouse was a master of the mother-in-law joke, and, even if you think it is a good idea to tell such a joke as part of a wedding speech, remember Bob was a professional comedian and knew exactly how it should be delivered within the context of the gathering. Now, I've never been to a comedian's wedding, but I suspect that any jokes would be delivered quite well – only because of many years of experience and probably because they wrote the gags themselves. Even if someone else wrote the material, it still takes a great deal of experience to know how to deliver it effectively and even then many jokes just simply fall flat on some audiences. If it's hard enough for a comedian to tell jokes and get laughs, think how difficult it is for you or me to do it – even if the audience is made up of people who already like you and who are virtually 'guaranteed' to laugh.

I know a number of top quality professional speakers, but the overwhelming majority *deliberately* do not tell jokes. Yet, many are considered to be extremely funny, even those who talk about quite weighty or serious subjects. My advice is to try to avoid jokes altogether. Tell stories and anecdotes instead. Real-life stories are unbeatable – but keep them clean!

TELLING STORIES

> Share a fact and I will learn. Share a truth and I might believe. Tell me a story and it will live in my heart forever.
>
> Anon

I believe that the key to good use of humour in wedding speeches is not to tell jokes, but to tell stories. And stories lend themselves well to weddings – the right sort of stories that is! We've all been to weddings where you just can't help thinking that the best man has stepped over a line. When that happens, it's not just unfunny, it's in poor taste and embarrassing for everyone – and I mean *everyone*. More often than not, the best man doesn't notice that people are embarrassed and just keeps on going oblivious to everyone's discomfort and laughing loudly at his own jokes.

QUICK TIP

If you are about to be a best man, please take this piece of advice. Do not under any circumstances tell risqué stories about the groom's past sexual exploits, even if he was a bit of a Jack the Lad. It may seem hysterically funny to you, but remember that your speech is for the benefit of the happy couple and the guests. The bride and groom will not be happy and the guests will not think you are either clever or funny. Sorry.

When it comes to humour, keep to safe territory – *a dull story told well will be much more memorable than a good joke told badly* – every time. And whilst I don't want you to bore the guests (see Chapter 4), I do want you to concentrate your efforts on stories and anecdotes as the main source of your humour.

Why are stories so effective?

We are all storytellers. We all live in a network of stories. There isn't a stronger connection between people than storytelling.

Marie Mosely, Professional Speaker and Broadcaster

Storytelling is an extremely powerful means of communication. By way of example, it is increasingly being used as a tool in business to help with areas such as sales, change management, scenario planning and maximising potential from mergers and acquisitions. It is effective because it helps management and employees to visualise different situations and to *see* potential benefits of taking different courses of action. Most communication in business connects with people at a cerebral, rational, intellectual and analytical level. But for people to see the benefits of what you are saying or suggesting, requires people to engage at a deeper, more emotional, human level. Telling stories achieves just this and so is the perfect medium to touch the hearts of people in a wedding speech.

Let's face it, other than the formal stuff you must say at a wedding, what you really want to do is touch people's hearts. Stories from real life are the most effective as they help people to connect with you and give them an insight into the lives of the people you are talking about – mainly the bride and/or groom. When you think about it, there has been a story leading up to the wedding day itself and most guests will want to hear something of how this happy union has come about.

QUICK TIP

'How they met' stories always go down well. Perhaps a particular guest was instrumental in the couple meeting – tell their story and touch the guests' hearts.

THE GOLDEN RULES

◆ Don't let your nerves spoil it for you and everyone else. The ceremony itself is the formal expression of love; the reception is the informal time. You might as well grab the opportunity with both hands and enjoy it!

◆ Try not to rely too much on notes and scripts as they interrupt the flow of your speech. What you say at a wedding is supposed to come from the heart – not three sheets of A4. Let it flow!

◆ Make it memorable by being different. Too many wedding speeches sound the same, so try to stand out from the crowd. Involve your guests, mention people by name, move around and help people to 'experience' your speech – not just hear it.

◆ Remember that humour is a universal communication tool. Use it but don't try to be a comedian. If you must tell jokes, practise on work colleagues over and over again until you get it right, but most important of all – be guided by their advice.

◆ Practise. Practise. Practise.

SUMMARY

In fact, there are no 'golden rules' to producing a great wedding speech. But if you recognise some of these key issues, you will turn, what is for many speakers the toughest part of the big day, into an enjoyable and memorable time for everyone. In the next chapter we look at the biggest sin of all – being boring. Yawn . . .

4

The Biggest Sin of All – Being Boring

bore (n) – *a person, thing or activity that wearies*
bore (v) – *to weary or annoy with tediousness*

The Chambers Dictionary

How would you feel if wedding guests described your speech as 'tedious' or 'annoying'? Unfortunately, it can and does happen.

We all know what Woody Allen meant when he said:

Eternity is a long time, especially towards the end.

How many of us have been a guest at a wedding and abruptly lost the will to live? I know I have – on more than one occasion. Eternity quickly becomes something very real and tangible, like quicksand sucking you under the surface. Until just moments ago you were having a great time, laughing out loud, wishing the happy couple well, meeting old friends, making new ones, enjoying the champagne and so on, and suddenly you wish it was all over. Wedding speeches can do that. The smile on your face starts to harden like plaster and you shift restlessly in your chair.

I attended a wedding last summer which had all the ingredients you would expect to find in a truly boring speech. The groom's speech was excellent – it was sincere, heartfelt, optimistic, short (thank goodness) and delivered with a cheery disposition. In short, perfect. My more critical comments are unfortunately reserved for the best man and the bride's father.

BEST MAN

He started by apologising for his lack of experience of speaking in public.

An apology at the beginning of a wedding speech always sets the tone for what is about to be received and has the effect of significantly lowering the guests' expectations for the next few minutes. This can be really disappointing for guests because to a certain extent they are expecting entertainment at this point in the proceedings. Whilst the honesty of the speaker is to be applauded, apologies at the beginning of any talk are just a cop out for poor preparation. If you tell the guests that it will be a bad speech, guess what will happen?

It was obvious that he had not rehearsed his speech.

How many times does this have to be said? Rehearse, rehearse, rehearse and then rehearse some more. Try to learn the first two or three paragraphs by heart and then revert to your prompts if you must use notes.

Not surprisingly, many people are nervous before making their speech, but several rehearsals will help enormously.

Speeches that have not been rehearsed also have the effect of irritating some audiences, which is not generally conducive to them enjoying themselves. Being slightly nervous is a good thing as nerves help to keep you focused on the job in hand and to moderate your behaviour. There is nothing worse than a best man on an ego trip – trust me.

His jokes were clearly downloaded from the internet.

We all tell jokes at work, at home or in the pub and get away with it probably because we heard someone else *tell it* to us in the first place. But there is something about repeating jokes that you find in a book or download from the web that just doesn't work. All jokes need a certain amount of movement, emphasis and animation to improve their delivery, and it's always that much more difficult to tell a joke well if you have only ever read it, rather than seen, heard and experienced it.

He was rude about the bride's mother (allegedly in fun).

Quite why anyone feels that they can get away with this at a wedding is beyond me. There is a time and place for banter with your mother-in-law, but at her daughter's wedding is not high up the list! Generally speaking, guests won't find it funny (you will hear a sharp intake of breath, like you do when a joke which is in very poor taste is told). It's just embarrassing, and embarrassment makes people switch off.

Much of his speech was about himself.

Anyone who talks about themselves unsolicited is generally boring. It's even more so at a wedding. The role of the best man is not to upstage the happy couple, and even if your life story is that interesting, no one wants to hear about it at the reception. Do everyone a favour and consider writing it in a book and then we can make up our own minds if we want to read it – not have it forced upon us.

He hardly mentioned the bride at all.

I won't dwell on this one too much because it's quite unusual for the bride not to be mentioned at her own wedding. But if you are reading this book because you are going to be a best man during the coming months, please take this tip and remember that at least half the guests are only really interested in the bride! Don't disappoint them.

He spoke for 37 minutes (I was counting).

37 minutes may not sound like a long time, but believe me it is. Don't go there.

QUICK TIP

There are some schools of thought that say the best man should speak for no more than four to ten minutes maximum. I take the view that you can speak for as long as the guests are enjoying themselves. However, unless you speak for a living, you can rarely sustain a great speech for longer than 20 minutes – and even then you will have to be very good for the guests to stay with you that long. Less is more. Keep it fun, succinct and sincere.

FATHER OF THE BRIDE

A speech in excess of 40 minutes.

As above! Anything over half an hour is dangerous territory. To make matters worse, the father of the bride almost always delivers the most sincere of the speeches, but as a result they can often come across as a bit too serious. And because the dads are so proud of their girls, there is also a tendency to go on rather too long.

QUICK TIP

My advice is to stick to a maximum of two well chosen and well told stories about your daughter and leave the reminiscing at that. Make one of the stories from her childhood, but one which features an aspect of her character that friends and guests are likely to recognise (for example, always late for things; very academic; very sporty; perhaps she's always been a bit of an entertainer). Make the other story from more recent years, again something that guests know her for or which perhaps includes the groom.

Again, remember that around half of the guests are more interested in the groom than the bride.

Too serious and too quietly spoken.

A wedding speech is a time for toasts, thank yous and celebration, but more often than not, brides' fathers deliver an address not dissimilar to a judge summing up in court. Having said that, this certainly is a big day for the bride's father and he's perfectly entitled to be serious in what he has to say.

However, in his attempt to be sincere, what often happens is that he will lower his voice and speak more slowly, making the guests have to strain to hear the sentiments. If these serious bits go on for much longer than a minute, you have lost the guests and they will quickly become bored.

Serious, heartfelt sentiments are a vital ingredient in great wedding speeches, but this does not mean that they have to be delivered with a solemn expression and gloomy demeanour. Guests are not averse to the serious bits, just as long as they can actually hear what is being said, they don't go on too long and the delivery is well paced.

It doesn't help either if the bride's dad stands with his back to the guests. But I have seen this happen all too often. Dads very often deliver their speech to the bride and groom, apparently forgetting the presence of their guests! Without a microphone it can be hard to hear the speeches at the best of times, let alone if the speaker is facing the wrong way!

QUICK TIP

If you have the opportunity to use a microphone, always take it. We don't need to go into microphone technique in this book other than to just say use one, but rest assured its use will make a big difference to the success of your speech.

Details of his daughter's Brownie interest badges.

I think you can probably work this one out for yourself! Yes, I have heard proud fathers listing their daughter's Brownie achievements, including her camping badge, artist's badge, circus performer badge, discovering faith badge, fire safety badge, Brownie cook (advanced) badge, cyclist badge, communicator badge (dad – please take note), First Aid (advanced) badge, Stargazer badge – to name just a few.

This is always quite a special moment for any guest at a wedding, resulting in a fine mixture of emotions fuelled by champagne. You don't know whether to cry with pride or with laughter. Certainly, it's a very special moment for the bride, normally evidenced by blushes so pink they match the upholstery of the chairs. If you are ever privileged to see this happen, just enjoy!

Details of his daughter's GCSE results (including grades).

Er, as above.

Naming all her boyfriends (we were spared the reasons for break ups).

Yes, some dads think this makes good content for their speech. Mind you, I was told recently about a wedding reception where the bride gave a speech in which, much to the amusements of the guests, she listed (and slated) all her new husband's ex girlfriends, two of whom were present. Tip: Don't go there.

HOW TO TELL IF THE GUESTS ARE BORED

In any situation where you are required to stand up and speak, it's important to remember that what you have to say is for the audience's benefit not yours. It follows that you would want to keep most of them awake, otherwise, to put it bluntly, you are wasting your and everyone else's time.

This may come as a surprise, but the best way to tell if the guests are awake is to actually look at them while you are speaking. Many best men, grooms and brides' dads *think* they are looking at people while they are speaking, but in fact are merely directing their gaze at people.

QUICK TIP

It's really important to actually look people in the eye; quite apart from aiding communication, you can see if people are still alive.

Good speakers 'feed off' the reactions of the guests, and constantly adjust the tone, pace and pitch of their speech. But most simply ignore them even when the evidence is right in front of them that they themselves have gone off the boil. Fidgeting is the main indication; if your guests are bored they may also be:

◆ shifting in their chairs

◆ crossing and uncrossing their legs

◆ crossing their arms

◆ looking around the room

◆ looking down

◆ scratching the back of their neck

- tapping or 'jogging' their feet up and down
- having glazed eyes
- surreptitiously waving and smiling to friends and relatives across the room
- whispering to the person next to them
- toying with cutlery (standing any unused knives, forks or spoons upright, with the end of the handle on the table or arranging them neatly on the table)
- rotating their wine glass by the stem
- putting their hand to their face (to cover a yawn).

So it's not as if there aren't plenty of clues to watch for! Tips for keeping guests alert include:

- keeping the speech short
- keeping it light, but passionate and sincere
- being animated and moving around a bit
- using a visual aid, perhaps to amplify a point
- smiling
- telling stories with real expression
- looking people in the eye and talking to them directly
- using people's names
- occasionally touching people.

THE DRUNK BEST MAN

I once attended a wedding where the best man was so nervous before his speech that he had 'one or two' whiskies for Dutch courage. One or two became three or four and before he knew it, he had used the word 'shit' to describe the groom's golf swing. Worse was to come.

This was a speech where there was little chance of the guests being bored. Our friend's speech nicely fulfilled the criteria of being light and was certainly sincere – evidenced by the fact that he told the groom he loved him more than his own family: 'I love you man . . . always have and always will.' He then kissed the groom in a warm embrace. Very touching.

As the fifth whisky surged through his veins and found its mark in what was left of his brain he moved to the subject of golf. Apparently he had played numerous games with Simon (the groom), had taken money off him on most occasions and was looking forward to future Saturday mornings when he would relieve him (and his lovely wife) of further funds. This was a dead certainty because Simon was 'completely and utterly shit at golf.' In fact: 'Simon couldn't hit a ball into a hole the size of fucking Watford. Ha, ha, ha.'

Tears rolled down the bride's face, the groom's face and my face, all for different reasons. A small number of guests literally jumped up and down in their seats thumping their tables in hysterics, while others smiled meekly and crossed their arms. From my perspective as the photographer it was great fun. I didn't know these people so wasn't particularly involved, but to relatives of the (unhappy) couple it was a disaster. Everyone wants their wedding day to be memorable, but for the right reasons.

SOME THOUGHTS ON ALCOHOL CONSUMPTION

As alcohol is absorbed, we all know that we become more talkative. Contrary to what you might think, this is the last thing you need if you are about to make a speech. Another side effect is that you can become boastful and slightly aggressive. You can only imagine what gems are likely to come out unintentionally.

As alcohol consumption increases further, motor coordination starts to be affected leading to slurring of speech and a staggering gait. I think most readers can imagine what happens next.

A low amount of alcohol will relax you, reduce tension and lower inhibitions, but even at these levels it does affect your attention and concentration. I'm not inclined to take a 'holier than thou' attitude, because it is a wedding after all. But clearly, too much alcohol is not particularly helpful – with boastfulness, aggression and slurring of words being characteristics not entirely conducive to the delivery of a great speech.

In the next chapter we will look at the ways to maximise the likelihood that you will be confident, prepared and ready for action!

FINAL THOUGHTS

The speeches are increasingly seen as one of the most important parts of the day. No longer are they solely a time for formal acknowledgements and 'thank yous'. Today, the guests want entertainment and action so make sure they get it!

To avoid putting the guests to sleep:

◆ Don't take your speech *too* seriously – remember you are not in court

◆ Keep it light but sincere

◆ Don't talk about yourself

◆ Smile as often as you can

◆ Look the guests in the eye

◆ Be animated

◆ Keep it short.

5

Rehearsing Your Speech

This chapter should be very short and ought to go something like this:

If you want your speech to be received well and you want to enjoy the experience – then **make sure you rehearse it**. Full stop.

There, I've said it.

But unfortunately, it's all too obvious that most wedding speeches are given little more rehearsal than a cursory run through in front of the shaving mirror on the day. And that includes the occasional bride's mother who jumps to her feet at the last minute. Whether you are the groom, the best man or the father of the bride you have a great deal to think about on the day, and whilst you know you should have given proper time to rehearsing your speech, somehow the shaving mirror rehearsal just doesn't seem to work. And never will.

My friend Kevin who was Head of Training for an insurance company and an expert on exam techniques once told me that there is absolutely no point in doing last minute 'cramming' on the day of an exam, because it makes no difference at all. If anything it could only serve to confuse you. The same is true for rehearsing your wedding speech. If you are going to do any rehearsal at all on the day, it should be to go over nothing more that your opening few lines, which ideally you will have already gone over many times before!

For this chapter, it wouldn't surprise me if you are expecting me to say: 'Learn your speech off by heart and practise it 28 times before the big day – without fail.'

Well, that could be one suggestion, but in the real world this won't always be possible. After all, many people have full-time jobs to go to and don't always have that much time to commit to their speech.

IMPROMPTU WEDDING SPEECHES

In fact, many of the best speeches I've seen at weddings appear to have been off the cuff. On investigation, many of them were – the table cloth bearing witness to a few hastily scribbled notes. This apparent 'devil may care' approach to your wedding speech can in fact be very effective. It's dangerous, but does also have its advantages:

◆ The guests are treated to what appear to be genuine, spontaneous and heartfelt sentiments.

◆ The pressure is taken off you as a speaker and so you say exactly how you feel at that moment, not what you think people will want to hear.

◆ If you consciously decide not to plan your speech in advance, it makes the run up to the day much more enjoyable. You will also find that you spend less of the actual marriage ceremony dreading the reception!

As a couple of words of caution on this approach, you may wish to make sure that you remember to thank everyone who needs to be thanked. People do like to be mentioned by name, and if you forget someone important there will be trouble. Also, many of the best speakers in the world succumb to stage fright, a sudden attack of nerves or 'dry mouth' can cause real problems if you have not prepared anything.

No rehearsal at all is a perfectly reasonable approach to your wedding speech. It's not to be recommended, but for many people it can and does work well. Just make sure that you make a conscious decision *in advance* of the wedding not to rehearse, rather than decide on the day itself!

REHEARSAL TECHNIQUES

Proper preparation and rehearsal is my preferred (and the safer) option. Though, as I mentioned earlier, it is reasonable to assume that most people will not have unlimited time available to practise their speech over and over again – particularly if you are the groom and happen to live with your bride-to-be. Most best men and grooms don't exactly put time aside for proper rehearsals, preferring the more informal setting of the golf course, squash court or pub to run through a few well chosen lines.

Wherever you choose, the important thing is that you do actually turn the speech over in your mind a number of times and wherever possible get used to the sound of your own voice speaking out loud. You can do this in the car, in the shower, when you are out running, cycling, walking the dog and so on. You don't have to have a quiet space – get some time to yourself when you can to say a few things out loud.

And the chances are that's all the time you will get – so make the most of it.

TIPS TO AID PREPARATION AND REHEARSAL

◆ Don't write out your speech long hand.

◆ Just jot down a few notes about what you would *like* to say, not what you are *going* to say. A few short, simple headings will suffice. For example, if you are the groom, your headings could be:

Welcome
Beautiful wife
First meeting
Scary parents
Holiday in Peru
Broken neck
Redundancy
Thank yous.

◆ Write down a few words for the stories (not jokes) that you want to tell. Again, don't write them out in full – just a couple of words. If a story is worth telling, you should be able to remember the details well without having to write it out.

- The jotting process is very important so write down more headings than you think you will need. It is unlikely that you will complete it in one session and you will often find that once you have started these notes, new ideas will pop into your head after you have had time to sleep on them.

- Always keep a notepad or some paper on you to catch ideas as they appear. I promise that once you have set your mind to the task, new ideas or topics will hit you at the least expected moment. Once you have written down everything you think you are going to talk about, make a point of not including anything else and stick to making the material you've got really good.

- Next, ruthlessly edit your notes to remove material that you know is simply not interesting enough. It may sound fascinating to you, but will the guests be interested? Start by ranking your headings in importance, beginning with 'must include' material.

- Rewrite what remains of your jottings in the form of a mind map® so that your notes take on some structure and form (see Chapter 8 and Resources at the end of the book).

Your mind map will form the basis of your speech. You are not obliged to use it on the day, but it should form the heart of your preparation and rehearsal. You will find that it provides you with a quick and easy reference point with which to help you remember the subjects you are going to cover and their order. It will be on one sheet of A4, extremely portable (so take it everywhere) and handy for referring to on a regular basis.

♦ In this way, you won't feel the need to do a full-scale dress rehearsal, and we can get you to the ideal point of delivering your speech without any notes at all, or at least with very few.

So it can be seen that I am advocating a fairly relaxed approach to preparation and rehearsal. I'm not saying don't do any (unless you consciously decide not to as described earlier), but what I am saying is don't lose sleep over it. I want you to enjoy your speech, so worrying too much about it will not be helpful.

As you will have limited time to put your speech together, these ideas are designed to help you make the most of the time that is available. Mind maps are a great way of organising your thoughts and, when combined with at least some time spent talking out loud in the shower, are a very effective way of getting you to the reception properly prepared.

If the complexities of your life are such that you really don't get *any* time to yourself to talk out loud there is another option, and one which I recommend to everyone.

VISUALISE YOURSELF DELIVERING A GREAT SPEECH

Now, I'm no expert on the inner workings and wonders of the human mind, but what I do know is that a superb way of rehearsing your speech is to do it 'in your head'. In fact, running through your speech in your mind can often be as effective a rehearsal as doing it for real.

The subconscious mind can't tell the difference between something that is real or something that is vividly imagined. If you vividly imagine yourself delivering your speech with confidence, flair, style, good humour and warmth, your execution on the day itself will reflect this because your mind will believe that it has had a 'real' rehearsal. Such 'creative visualisation' (one of the best resources is *Creative Visualization* by Shakti Gawain) is extremely powerful as a rehearsal tool and has the additional benefit of being possible at a moment's notice and at virtually any time of the day or night.

Unlike real rehearsals, you can do these mental practice sessions as often as you want. And every session will be of benefit however short.

TIPS ON VISUALISATION REHEARSALS

♦ Start by vividly imagining how you will feel as you sit down after giving your speech.

♦ Make a conscious effort to imagine what it will be like and how good you will feel as all the guests applaud loudly and enthusiastically.

♦ Imagine several people patting you firmly on the back as they congratulate you and others giving you the thumbs up from tables across the room.

♦ See their faces as they tell you what a great speech it was. Listen to the words they use and feel yourself smiling broadly and being proud of your fantastic achievement.

♦ Now, rewind this 'film' in your mind to the start of your speech and see yourself rising to your feet.

◆ You feel relaxed, confident and are looking forward to talking to the guests. You already know that they are going to enjoy your speech and will applaud loudly.

◆ See and hear yourself speaking in your mind's eye. See yourself looking guests in the eye and feel the warmth of their response in return.

◆ See the guests nodding, smiling and enjoying themselves and imagine how that will make you feel.

Come the moment of truth, you will be amazed at how what you imagined beforehand magically comes to life. In short, creative visualisation is a superb tool for both building your confidence and getting vital rehearsal time.

FINAL THOUGHTS

Rehearsal is the most important thing you can do before a speech as it helps with so many different aspects:

◆ Your confidence and nerves

◆ Planning

◆ Helping you decide the format for your notes

◆ Knowing what you are going to say

◆ Knowing how you are going to say it.

Additionally, sometimes an idea for your speech may sound great in principle, but simply doesn't work when said out loud on the day. Even if you only get time for one rehearsal it will, if nothing else, help you to decide what to leave out.

It is often what you *don't* say that can make the biggest difference to a wedding speech. Best men – please note.

In Part Two we arrive at the big day itself.

Part Two
The Big Day

6

Presentation is Everything

Your wedding speech would not normally be considered the most appropriate time to make a business pitch or presentation. Yet I have witnessed this twice, and on both occasions there were lessons that other less commercially minded grooms, best men and brides' fathers could learn when making their wedding speech.

Whilst I have never been subjected to a full blown PowerPoint business presentation at any of them, I have heard many speeches which have included subtle business messages in some shape or form – either for businesses belonging to friends and family or outright plugs for their own. At one wedding I attended, an enterprising couple persuaded a patisserie to 'sponsor' their wedding cake in return for an enthusiastic mention in the groom's speech. Whilst on other occasions I have returned home from the reception with a very nice paperweight branded with the colours of an upmarket estate agent and a glossy corporate brochure about my new local replacement window service.

THE STORY OF JIM AND LAURA

A happy couple, let's call them Jim and Laura, took full advantage of the 'platform time' and in an excellent joint speech told all their friends and relatives about their exciting new business venture – treating us to the economic benefits of a draught-free home (which naturally they could provide). Their pitch to an apparently target market of, er, close friends and relatives was surprisingly well rehearsed, well delivered and indeed well received.

Jim started his speech by thanking his bride's father for providing such a lovely spread, lovely daughter and a lovely business partner. After thanking his guests for their delightful wedding presents he got into his stride:

> Our philosophy at Jones' Window Solutions is one of excellence in design, excellence in delivery and excellence in service.

Excellent. Reassured that we wouldn't be able to match such quality at a cheaper price elsewhere in the county, the coming minutes revealed that the window frames were fully welded (as opposed to mechanically jointed), had high thermal insulation, excellent noise reduction and enjoyed a full ten year guarantee. We were also guaranteed to save £171.40 a year on our heating bills.

The guests were impressed. Clearly such remarkable benefits were unheard of in the world of replacement windows and the young couple were to be commended for their industriousness. Aunties, uncles, cousins and even six and eight year old nephews were seen nodding appreciatively as the glossy brochures (complete with 10% discount voucher) were distributed around the tables. It would go down well with the wedding cake. I waited for the line about 'Buy today and save a further 20%' but (sadly) it never came.

What was most interesting about Jim and Laura's speech was the confidence with which it was delivered. They were on their pet subject and so felt particularly comfortable talking about it. They had approached their speech in an efficient businesslike manner and it had paid off. As I said earlier, a business presentation is not normally what you expect at a wedding, but strangely it worked very well. Not only did it work, it will have been remembered for years to come and I have no doubt they will have got business from it.

FINAL THOUGHTS

Presentation is everything and a great way to approach your wedding speech is in a businesslike manner. Plan it, prepare it, organise your material and deliver it with confidence, clarity and conviction. My advice is not to turn your wedding speech into an advertisement for your business, but to adopt the same organised and methodical approach to it.

In the next chapter, we look closer at building your confidence before your wedding speech.

(7)

Confidence and Relaxation

As we mentioned in Chapter 1, making a speech or a presentation in public is one of the scariest things you can ever do – apparently more so than death or bungee jumping (or both). For many people reading this book, 'fear' and 'nerves' will be the biggest issues for them. I hope this chapter will help you to understand that these are not only entirely natural, but in fact helping you to perform at your best.

WHO GETS THE MOST NERVOUS?

The best man? The groom? The father of the bride? Well, each does, but for different reasons. The groom is having a roller-coaster ride of a day of emotions and the speech is just something else on the agenda. I don't mean to trivialise it, but the one person who you would really expect to be nervous, is often the most relaxed when it comes to the speeches.

Many grooms have told me that all they want to do at the reception is to try to relax, stand back and take in and remember as much as possible of this special day. After all the lead up and preparation, the day itself will just fly by so many grooms make a conscious effort to slow it down. This can have a very calming effect and will actually make them less nervous than others come the speeches.

The best man is seen by many as the entertainer for the day – the clown, the court jester. Whilst he has formal duties to perform, his speech often reveals a side to the groom that many of the guests have never seen before. And great fun it is. Many best men are chosen because they are natural performers, but due to this heavy responsibility, they will be very nervous and often most susceptible to the attractions of the bar!

As far as the father of the bride is concerned, I have yet to give away my own beautiful daughter Isobel, as thankfully Jake from the *Tweenies* is currently the man in her life. However, the day will doubtless arrive, and I'll update this section when I know how it feels to make that particular speech. I have my suspicions that the feelings of nerves will be for very different reasons.

Whilst the father of the bride's speech is an important moment for any dad, it is also worth remembering that, other than the toastmaster, master of ceremonies or a brief introduction from the best man, he is on first – traditionally the slot for the 'warm up man'. We mentioned earlier that the dad's speech often comes over as the most sincere of the three possibly due to maturity and/or the significance of the moment for him, but he should try to remember that as the first speaker, he will set the tone and scene for what is to come.

TACKLING THOSE NERVES

Pick up any book on presentation skills and you will find there's usually a chapter or section on 'handling butterflies'. Get real! We all know it neither feels like nor has anything to do with the delicate and fragile wing flutterings of Lepidoptera. If we're honest, it feels more like you're going to violently throw up after having been kicked in the stomach!

Regular speakers will tell you that the *most* nerve-racking speeches you can give are to people you know well. So, making a speech at your wedding has to rank at the top of the charts in terms of nerve-inducing moments – and what a shame given that your wedding day is supposed to be the happiest day of your life!

Times have changed a great deal since we lived in caves, where if we found ourselves in a stressful situation, we generally had two choices – fight or run. Today's society considers that neither is an appropriate choice for most circumstances, leaving us with the third choice – grin and bear it. This doesn't stop the stress building inside us and so affects our ability to think clearly and to perform tasks properly. For many people, the thought of having to give a speech at their wedding can turn an already nervous person into a quivering wreck. This can result in just a little too much alcohol being consumed making matters only worse.

If you are the groom, there will be relatives of your new wife whom you may not have met before and who will be scrutinising your every word for clues to your character, your trustworthiness and (let's face it) the size of your wallet. And to be sure, they will pick up from your speech all the clues they need to tell them everything they want to know about you – without you even realising it!

Your speech is a direct reflection of you, your personality, your honesty, dependability, responsibility, reliability, credibility and yes, perhaps your virility and fidelity too. They will base their perception of you on everything they see and hear during those few minutes of your wedding speech, so consider this book as an additional aid to family harmony.

TIPS TO HELP BUILD YOUR CONFIDENCE

Pretend you are confident

Clues to lack of confidence include not smiling, a quiet voice and hunched posture. Clues to nervousness include mumbling, speaking too fast or too slowly, too softly or too loudly, stuttering, going red, fiddling with change in your pocket, getting extremely hot and sweating. And then of course there is the dreaded 'dry mouth'.

It's worth remembering that in everyday conversation a lot of this also happens, but it doesn't really matter that much and no one minds to the extent that it is actually a problem. Some people are naturally shy but very often their communication skills can be improved dramatically through increased self-esteem.

QUICK TIP

Even if you are not feeling very confident, pretend that you are. By acting self-assured and confident, guests will perceive you to be so. Within a few moments you will believe it yourself.

Use famous quotations in your speech

Using quotes in any presentation, talk or speech is a great trick to make you sound more confident than you really are. Including a couple of well chosen and relevant quotes makes you *look* like you know what you are talking about or have at least made some preparation. (You will find some useful quotations featured at the end of Chapter 15.)

Look out for people you know well

If it is your wedding, then hopefully this should come quite easily. But try to find people who you know *really* well such as your closest friends. A friendly face in a crowd is like a lighthouse in a storm. It provides reassurance when you are 'all at sea'.

On the subject of looking out for people, many speakers ask me where they should look when they are speaking to their guests. Some say you should pick a spot at the back of the room and keep your gaze fixed squarely on it. This approach does have the merit of helping you to get your volume and pitch right, but many guests find this a little disconcerting after a while, and start to wonder what is so interesting behind them. These are the people sneaking a look over their shoulder wondering if perhaps the police are standing there. Also by taking this approach you may look like you've just come off a wedding speech course, which has the effect of making you appear wooden, stilted and even unfriendly.

QUICK TIP

My advice is to address everyone in the room as you speak. Face people on all sides by moving your body and head around, taking in as many people as possible. Look as many of them as you can *in the eye*. Wherever possible, try to smile broadly – you'll be amazed at how many will smile back at you, which in turn will do wonders for your confidence.

Go on – smile if it kills you!

Smiling has a remarkable effect on anyone making a speech and indeed their audience. Not only does it show people how happy you are, but it has an infectious effect on your guests. It will also make you feel good and before long you will be having a great time. It is possible of course to smile too much, so that you start to look like some crazed madman in a horror film. Try to smile at people as you would when having a conversation with a really good friend.

In other words, aim to be friendly, welcoming, sociable, warm and natural. If you *look* as though you are relaxed and confident, your guests will respond as though you are, which will make you feel even more confident. Smiling and laughing has an additional benefit in that it exercises your larynx and has a warming effect on the tone of your voice.

QUICK TIP

A useful workout for the larynx before your speech is to say 'ng' (as in king) up and down like a siren. It's probably best to take yourself off somewhere private first, but this little exercise is extremely effective in getting your voice into gear before you get to your feet.

Talk out loud

Saying 'ng' up and down like a siren is also effective as it gets you to talk out loud. Many people who have never spoken in public are often quite startled at the sound of their own voice the first time they hear it at the pitch needed to address a room full of people. Even when talking to a small group of guests (say 20 people), it can be quite unnerving. To a group of 150 people or more, it can be quite a big shock and often, even the most confident of people are taken aback when they hear their own voice. Usually it is the last thing they are expecting to surprise them on the day.

QUICK TIP

You can also try humming and singing in the shower or car. The important point is to get used to the sound of your own voice, preferably done regularly over the few weeks before the wedding and definitely on the day itself.

Look the part

It never ceases to amaze me just how many grooms and their best men have 'loosened their clothing' by the time it comes for their speeches. Whether the dress code for the wedding is very formal or a little more relaxed, it is very important that those making speeches maintain their polished look for as long as possible. I have found that those who remove their jacket, roll up their sleeves or undo their top button before their speech, tend to look less prepared, less confident and more uneasy at the prospect.

Some might say that taking off their jacket makes them feel more relaxed, and this is fair enough. It's just that you don't look the part for making a speech. And of course presentation is everything – as is perception.

In short – look the part!

Rehearse

Let's say it again for good measure. Practising your speech is the single most effective way of increasing your confidence. If nothing else, you will at least have a vague idea of what you are going to say and you might even be able to remember what you are going to say next. Practising also reduces your need for notes and a well rehearsed speech will make you look much more sincere too.

QUICK TIP

When practising your speech at home do it much louder, 'bigger' and more exaggerated than you would actually deliver it. In other words, practise your speech at a volume level and pitch, which you would normally find quite uncomfortable or embarrassing, and you will find that on the day you will hit exactly the right pitch for your guests.

Boost your feeling of authority

Michaela Kennen is an outstanding voice coach in London who once told me an excellent tip for boosting your confidence, authority and control of the room. Michaela suggests imagining a circle around you, perhaps like a hoop. This roughly represents the amount of space which you normally occupy.

Now, imagine the circle or hoop growing around you until it is two metres in diameter and try to feel what it's like to take up that amount of space. You actually begin to feel that you have greater confidence and control of the room. Next, take it a step further and imagine the circle reaching all sides of the room – now you really are in control!

QUICK TIP

If possible, do this before everyone comes into the room or the venue for your reception. A few moments of quiet and personal time doing this exercise will make a huge difference to your confidence when standing in front of the guests.

Remember that we all make speeches every day without realising it

It's quite possible that by making a point of highlighting the scary aspects of speaking in public, that we are making an unnecessarily big deal of the occasion. We make unrehearsed speeches all the time as we each go about our daily business and activities. Communicating with other humans actually comes very easily to most people and we do it without even trying. In fact, many of us can talk passionately and entertainingly for hours and hours without fear, notes or rehearsal.

Keep this in mind as you think about your wedding speech. Communication by talking is the most natural thing on earth and we all do it every day of our lives with very little effort at all.

HOW TO RELAX BEFORE YOUR SPEECH

You will remember from earlier in this chapter that we talked about how the body deals with stressful situations: we deal with it assertively and proactively, or we get out of there quick. Either way, when we are facing a difficult, stressful or frightening situation, our body reacts and adrenaline gushes into our bloodstream. And we all know what that feels like as our heart beats harder and you feel ever so slightly unwell!

But most inexperienced speakers misinterpret these unnerving feelings as a problem or hindrance. In fact, these feelings are actually helping to sharpen us up in order that we deal with the situation effectively and efficiently and perform to the best of our ability. Many professional speakers find the feelings extremely unpleasant as well, but the difference is that they understand and accept the sensation as the body working *for us*, not against us.

If you can tell yourself that the, often overwhelming, feeling of nerves is actually helping you, then your actions, behaviour and movements become much more fluid and relaxed. The words begin to flow and you begin to enjoy yourself. This is what is happening when you hear actors, performers, speakers or sports stars say they have learned how to control their nerves to their advantage before a performance or an important sporting event.

In a similar vein, I believe it's important to remember that although you (whether the groom, best man or father of the bride) feel it's really important to put on a good speech (which is what creates the pressure), it is after all a very happy day. And because it is such a happy occasion, you can afford to relax ('be cool' as my son would say) and enjoy yourself. This is a moment for celebration, not for accounting for your performance and actions to the board of directors or defending yourself in court. The guests are not putting you on trial, they are there to enjoy themselves.

Many people forget this as they rise to make their speech, and in so doing, miss out on the enormous enjoyment that can be had from welcoming, thanking and celebrating with their friends, relatives and guests.

MORE TIPS TO MAKE YOU FEEL RELAXED AND COMFORTABLE

Breathe

Breathing is good. The act of breathing takes in oxygen, which ends up in our blood and helps us to do everything we need to do each day. When we get wound up about something like a difficult task or a stressful situation, our breathing can become faint. This strikes me as self-defeating. It follows that in stressful situations we would benefit from more oxygen, so steady, deep breaths help us enormously, particularly when combined with a conscious effort to relax.

QUICK TIP

If you are starting to feel anxious or panicky before your speech, take yourself off to the loos, shut the door behind you and breathe slowly and deeply for two or three minutes.

This won't necessarily remove the feelings of nervousness (remember that nerves are actually helping you), but it will ease them as well as easing tension in your shoulders and throat. You will also feel calmer and much more ready and prepared to do your stuff.

A breathing exercise

Just as long, slow deep breaths can be really helpful, so too can shorter puffs. No, I'm not advocating the use of dodgy cigarettes. What I am suggesting is that you try breathing in and out (as above), but this time concentrating on the exhale. I have two exercises which I use:

1. As you breathe out say the letter 'f' for about 5 seconds as in 'ffffffff'. Repeat this three or four times.

2. Imagine you are trying to blow out one of those joke birthday candles. Gently try to blow out the candle up to 20 times with short puffs every half second.

Make happy memories work for you

Our minds can have a very powerful effect on our behaviour. If we wake up in the morning, trip over the cat, can't find the shirt we wanted to wear, it's raining and the post is full of bills, we expect the rest of the day to be as bad. Equally, if we wake up, spring out of bed and the sun is shining we believe it's going to be a great day!

Our subconscious mind is constantly talking to us and telling us how to feel, and we've already seen how positive visualisation and talk can boost self-esteem and get us through just about any situation. At the same time, we can also use positive and happy memories to make us feel good, and many people find this a really good way of perking them up when they are nervous about something or feeling down. This can work before your wedding speech as well if you spend a moment or two remembering perhaps a past success or maybe a happy family moment. You will find yourself smiling as you remember something and this instantly makes you feel good.

Take a walk

Taking a quick walk round the car park or up and down the back stairs is often given as advice to people who are nervous before making a business presentation. It helps to release nervous tension and gets the blood flowing. Whether it's practical advice at your wedding reception is another matter, but if you think it could help you, then give it a try. If you are the groom, just tell your new wife what you are doing before you head off to the car park!

Avoid caffeine

I love extremely strong, dark coffee and some years ago I was given a coffee maker (a wedding present as it happens). I took myself off to the local specialist coffee merchant and asked for the darkest, strongest beans they had on the premises. The owner, a mature, heavily tanned gentleman with a gold tooth, flashed a glance at me wickedly and whispered: 'Oh yes, sir, I have just the thing for you.' A minute later he emerged with a small barrel on his shoulder. It was black, covered with cobwebs and he looked like a pirate about to do something nasty with dynamite.

'I think you'll like this, sir. Half a pound was it?'

'Er, yes, thank you,' I replied apprehensively. The grinding process completed, I walked home clutching my precious cargo.

The following morning, my coffee maker was duly put through its paces and I was delighted by the rich, heady but sweet aroma of my mystery coffee. In fact, it was superb and I had three very strong mugfulls. This set me up nicely for the day; a day which included a sales presentation in Bagshot, Surrey at 11.30am.

I met up with a colleague at 10.45am and we enjoyed a rather bland cappuccino. However, there was enough caffeine in the frothy drink to tip me over the coffee equivalent of the drink–drive limit. The shakes took hold, my knees went to jelly, I started to see double and my mouth went numb. My colleague Mike, sensing that something was wrong, took hold of my arm and steered me out of the café, clearly embarrassed that the staff might think I was drunk. The sensations of overdosing on caffeine were not dissimilar and I did not relish the thought of having to make the presentation. Mike saved the day.

In short, any amount of tea or coffee (however small) can impair your ability to make a speech. Try to avoid it if you can. Unfortunately, in a valiant attempt to stay sober for the speeches, I know a number of people who have stuck rigidly to tea or coffee throughout the morning. But by the time they make their speech, they have had the best part of ten cups, which can have much the same affect as if they had been drinking champagne.

So I'm conscious that we're getting to the point where you are being advised practically not to do *anything* on the big day which might spoil your speech. You can't even have a cup of tea or coffee now! Like all things – moderation is the key.

SURVIVING THE WORST CASE SCENARIO

So you have planned, prepared and practised. You've been saying your speech out loud for the last week, you've drunk nothing but mountain spring water and you've been for a brisk walk round the block. You've blown out your imaginary candles, visualised expanding hoops, you're smiling, brimming with confidence . . .

. . . and nothing happens. You open your mouth to utter those first few carefully planned words:

My wife and I . . .

. . . and your voice freezes. In fact, it feels like your whole brain has frozen. The first moments of panic start to hit you and all you can do is see the faces of your guests smiling back at you as you struggle for the words, air, inspiration – anything!

So what? It doesn't matter.

FINAL THOUGHTS

If you make a mistake, nerves get the better of you or you can't remember what you were going to say – it doesn't matter. Nobody minds. Stop, compose yourself, make light of your misfortune (don't apologise) and start again. In fact, people will warm to you. British guests particularly will inwardly feel slightly embarrassed at first (that's their problem, not yours) and just as quickly will be mentally willing you on.

You will quickly regain confidence after your false start and get into your stride. And guess what? Immediately after you sit down you will feel elated.

And so begins your new career in public speaking.

8

Scripts, Notes and Cue Cards

A wedding speech should not just be a list of people who need thanking, but all too often that is precisely what happens. I don't really have a problem with that, as long as there is something else for people to hear – like terms of affection, undying love for each other or your daughter, how the bride and groom met in the stationery cupboard at work and so on. You know the sort of thing! However, when a wedding speech does just consist of a list of people to thank, it does not come as a surprise when a large sheet of paper is removed from the inside jacket pocket, unfolded ceremoniously, and read out. I cringe when this happens.

It's nice for the named individuals to hear themselves being mentioned, but can be a little dull for everyone else. A really good wedding speech has substance, style, passion and sincerity, and occasionally a dash of creativity.

Substance, style, passion, sincerity and creativity are very difficult to get across from a sheet of paper or cue cards. For this to happen, the speech almost has to be performed rather than read. And the only way this performance will come to life is if it is rehearsed and practised, and then rehearsed again (and again). But let's be realistic – it doesn't always happen that way does it? We know we would all *like* to rehearse our speeches thoroughly, but other commitments just get in the way of our best intentions. So all too often we resort to using notes.

I've been speaking to groups of people in business for over 26 years and still use back-up notes. I take them to every talk I give and leave them where I can see them. I can do the talk without referring to them, but just having the notes to hand makes me feel more confident – just in case they are needed.

Ideally, a wedding speech should follow a similar format. You already know who you want to thank, and it is a good idea to have the names available if you happen to forget them at the crucial moment. But having your whole speech written out in full is a different matter altogether. I'm hoping that this book will give you sufficient tips and ideas to let you believe that you really can do it without a full script, but if you must then it's not the end of the world, just a bit tedious for all the guests.

The main problem with using scripts is that it reduces the amount of eye contact you have with the guests, and this in turn reduces the perceived sincerity of your speech. Just look at any politician to see what I mean.

MY TIPS FOR USING NOTES

1. Start by writing an extensive outline of what you would like to say. Include within your notes a few keywords that

will remind you of any stories or anecdotes that you would like to tell, for example, 'Spain'. Don't write out the stories; just put down your keywords.

2. Next, remove about a third of everything you have written down. Cut it down to the really good stuff.

3. Then, read through what is left four or five times so that you start to become familiar with the material.

4. Reorder things so that they come in a logical progression. Think about what would fit well at the beginning, middle and end of the speech. Don't just think of a list of things to say which start when you stand up and finish when you have run out of things to say. Try to put the best bits at the beginning and the end.

5. Read through it all again another four or five times, removing anything else that you do not think is strong enough. Try to make sure that what you have included will be interesting to the *majority* of the guests, leaving out anything that may be hysterical only for you and a couple of other people in the know.

6. Finally, reduce any paragraphs or long sentences to just a couple of phrases, so that your speech material become a series of short notes and keywords.

Transfer these short notes to one side of a piece of A4 or no more than four postcard size pieces of card. Number the cards in the bottom right hand corner in case you drop them. Type the notes onto the paper or cards using Times New Roman with an 18pt font size. This will make them easier to read when you deliver your speech.

Reducing the speech to just a few words that you are now familiar with will force you to articulate what you want to say, but with the reassurance of some notes to support you if you get lost.

If you use more than one side of A4 or more than four cards, your speech will be too long.

MIND MAPS®

You may remember that we mentioned mind maps earlier in this book and it is worth going into these a little further. Mind maps are another excellent way of writing down your speech, but in a way which forces you to speak rather than read. They are used extensively in business and those who use mind maps find them an excellent way of graphically organising their thoughts and messages into a logical sequence. (I have included an example of a mind map in the Resources section of this book.)

Mind maps have the added advantage of being very visual, which many speakers find beneficial because they utilise graphics, pictures, words and colours. They are particularly effective in the planning and recalling of a speech, and by using these different elements they are able to contain large amounts of information. In a nutshell, mind maps help you to easily find what you want to say, whilst at the same time making the information memorable.

My only criticism of them in the context of a wedding speech is that, because of their graphical nature, everyone can see that you are using one and many people will comment as such to you, perhaps even wanting to take a closer look after your speech. But on balance, the advantages of mind maps far outweigh any disadvantages. (Further information on mind maps can be found in the Resources section.)

FINAL THOUGHTS

Using notes, scripts and cue cards is purely a matter of personal preference. You have to balance the advantages of their use, with what you will lose – which will almost always be the natural flow of a good speech,.

There is still no better way of remembering what you are going to say and keeping the flow of your speech going than by having several rehearsals. Rehearsals will help to build your confidence and style, and then your notes can be used as short prompts to keep you on track.

Part Three
Be Yourself

9

The Father of the Bride

*'Marriage has its ups and downs, Stephen and
Catherine. I wish you health, wealth and happiness for
the future, and if nothing else, I hope you will be
happier than my wife and I have been!'*

Anon.

The father of the bride's speech is the moment where, as
Rowan Atkinson said in his famous sketch, 'the man who
paid for the damn thing is allowed to speak a word or two
of his own.' In days gone by, the cost of the wedding was
often in direct proportion to the length of the bride's father's
speech. Today, the bride's father is (mercifully) not always
called upon to pay for the whole thing himself. The shape
and structure of the family is changing so much that several
people may help to fund the ever increasing cost of the
wedding, thus limiting dad's right to hog the time for the
speeches.

Once, when I was taking photographs at a wedding in leafy
Dorking in Surrey, I had finished the pictures of the bride
and groom outside the church, and turning to the guests I
asked for the parents to join us for a group shot. Nine people
stepped forward – six men and three women. Work that one
out if you can.

Fortunately, only three of the men claimed to be the bride's father, as evidenced by their three speeches later on. Even after they had all spoken (for 25 minutes each), I was, and still am blissfully unaware of how the bride had three dads (or was it six?).

THE GENERAL ROLE OF THE FATHER OF THE BRIDE

We discovered in Part One that the bride's father has the role of proposing a toast of health and happiness to the happy couple. He will also welcome the groom's parents, all the guests and, like it or not, the groom to his family. As he goes through his list, it is at this point he realises the bar bill will significantly exceed his usual round at the local.

And this, for most fathers will be a moment of high emotion. Not because of the bar bill I hasten to add, but for other, more obvious reasons. I have noticed that more often than not, the father of the bride's speech tends to be the most sincere and earnest of the three. Perhaps this comes with a few more years' maturity, but these speeches tend to fall into two categories – 'the quiet and emotional' or the 'loud and stiff upper lip'.

DAD NO. 1: MR QUIET

On this great day, you are, after all, extremely proud of your girl, but know in your heart that life must move on. You want all your guests to know how proud you are, and your speech is as good a time as any to tell everyone. But as we discovered earlier in the book, we don't need to hear about her GCSE results.

Anyone who does not regularly speak in public tends to be a bit on the quiet side and this can become over emphasised if you are talking about the tricky business of handing over your daughter to another man. And of course, there isn't a man on the whole planet who will be good enough for her.

PRIVATE MOMENTS

If you are an inexperienced or nervous dad, it can often be very difficult to express how you feel. You know you want to say something loving to your daughter, but it can feel uncomfortable saying it in front of a large gathering. My advice for this situation is to say your private words in private. Take your daughter to one side before your speech and tell her exactly how you feel, how proud you are and so on. Many dads have much that they *want* to say in their speech. Indeed, they have probably thought about this moment many times over many years, but come the big moment, they can't quite bring themselves to say it in front of so many people. They bottle it and sometimes regret it for years.

It is easy to understand why this happens, so say your private words *before* your speech, and then stick to a couple of well chosen childhood or teenage stories for the bulk of your speech. You could even get your daughter to help you with the content by coming up with some of her own memories.

QUICK TIP

Make sure you know the stories inside out and back to front so that you don't have to refer to notes. As you start to speak, have a private wink to your daughter to reinforce the love that you feel.

Wherever possible, face the guests, look as many people as possible in the eye (or at least in their general direction if you are very nervous) and smile as you talk. The result will be a speech where the guests feel part of a happy family moment and where your daughter has shared an even more private moment with her loving father.

DAD NO. 2: MR EMBARRASSING

Where's the enemy sitting?

And so began the speech of one father of the bride who wanted to remain anonymous for the purposes of this book. But nevertheless, a cracking start and one guaranteed to get everyone's attention! Particularly the groom's relatives.

You can see how he thought this would be funny. It certainly has the *potential* to be so, but to use a line like this requires you to be a master of comedy, which most of us are not! This was a classic example of nerves controlling our mouth rather than our brains. It's the 'it seemed a good idea at the time' scenario.

All too often, nerves can have exactly the opposite effect from making a speaker go quiet or hesitant and cause them to behave very strangely. The volume levels go up, the face goes red, and the dad bellows his speech to his shell-shocked guests. The subject matter too can often be a little surprising, not to say embarrassing for his daughter. For example, I recently heard about a father who, towards the end of his speech, turned and said to his daughter:

> And now, Samantha, I have something very special for you.
> I hope you and your children will treasure it for many years
> to come.

Reaching overdramatically into his jacket pocket, he produced a small red box, which resembled a ring box.
Samantha beamed with anticipation, wondering if this might
be a family heirloom. She was wrong!

> First, I'm going to have to let you into a little secret – I think
> you are old enough now. I'm sorry to have to tell you that
> when you were a little girl, it wasn't the tooth fairy who left
> you money under your pillow. It was me!

Not entirely sure where this was going, Samantha grinned
awkwardly with one of those smiles that was a fusion of
'let's humour him' and 'please stop – NOW'.

Blundering on regardless, dad continued excitedly: 'I have
kept this all these years for this moment – and now you can
have it back!' As dad carefully and proudly opened the small
box, the guests leaned eagerly forward to catch a glimpse of
the contents – one small child's tooth. As if in oral sympathy
with Samantha's father, the guests sighed a collective
'Aaah'.

Not entirely knowing where to look, Samantha gaped for a
moment in astonishment at her now extremely proud father.
Unfortunately, her dad hadn't finished. Reaching into a
different pocket, he took out a brown dog-eared envelope.
Samantha winced at the thought that he was about to present
her with the remaining nineteen of her baby teeth.

It was almost as bad.

Turning to the guests, her father carefully opened the envelope and removed a piece of pink notepaper:

> I have here, ladies and gentlemen, one of Samantha's letters to the tooth fairy. I thought you would like to listen to a couple of extracts . . .

I will spare you the contents of the letter. Needless to say that whilst her father felt this tribute said everything that needed to be said about his love for his daughter, his guests' emotions ranged from hysterics to awkwardness and embarrassment for the poor girl.

In short – don't embarrass your daughter. Before you open your mouth, think very carefully about what you are going to say, and just ask yourself, 'Will my daughter be OK with this?'

There is one subject however which has the potential to embarrass her, but in a fun way and to which she is unlikely to take offence, and this is to mention her skills with a credit card. This *always* goes down well with the guests and will also get a laugh from the happy couple.

TIPS FOR THE FATHER OF THE BRIDE

Act as the warm up man

A good tip is to suggest that the groom or best man will soon be 'entertaining us' or 'treating us to their words of wisdom' or something similar. This creates an air of expectation and anticipation amongst the guests, and to some extent takes the pressure off the bride's father with the implication that 'the best is yet to come'. I've already said that it is not a good idea to say things like 'Unaccustomed as I am to public speaking' or 'I'm not very used to this' or to put your speaking skills down, but it's possible to say much the same thing by hinting that the best speakers are coming later.

Introductory remarks

This is the relatively easy bit, where you can beam proudly at the assembled group and say how you feel. Yes, it really is that easy! Subjects you talk about which will make you look like a seasoned professional speaker include:

The weather

Confirm what everyone already knows by saying what a lovely day it is, or how disappointing it is that the photos had to be taken under umbrellas. Either way, everyone will agree with you.

The guests

Welcome the guests and say how nice it is to see everyone. Try to mention anyone who has had to travel a long way – they will appreciate it and like you even more for it.

So far so good

Assuming everything has gone to plan, say how well everything is going so far. Say what a lovely or moving service it was at the church or register office, comment on any nice remarks that were made by either the minister or the registrar – and again you will find that everyone agrees with you.

So you will have gathered that the trick here is to make relaxed comments about things that people agree on. Do this right from the very start. It is a useful speaker's ploy which helps to get everyone onside straight away.

Welcome the groom's family
Part of the father of the bride's duties is to welcome the groom to his family, and the groom's parents to the wedding celebrations. Of course, most of us are unable to choose our friends, but the marriage of your daughter becomes one of those occasions when new friends are 'forced' upon you.

Part of your speech should be dedicated to talking about the groom and his parents and to saying how genuinely pleased you are to have met them all. This will go a long way to oiling the wheels of inter-family relationships for at least the next few months. If you really aren't too keen on the groom's family, then at least sing the praises of the groom himself as this will be received well by everyone from his side of the family. Again, if you are aware that a long lost relative of his has come a long way, make a point of highlighting it.

Get the groom's name right
And, for that matter, the names of the guests. In researching this book, I was quite surprised to discover just how many people had reported that the bride's father got the name of the groom wrong. As you can imagine, this has potential for embarrassment for a number of people – not least of whom will be the bride, the groom and (when he realises his mistake) the bride's father.

On the plus side, this does tend to get a good laugh.

Confusion with names can cause all sorts of problems at weddings. At my own, for example, my wife's uncle arrived a third of the way through the reception having been caught in traffic. He was naturally feeling a little stressed and embarrassed as he sat down at our table, whereupon he started introducing himself to those he had not previously met.

The first person he introduced himself to was my best man Paul. A handsome man in his early forties. Having not met Paul before and not knowing that he was my best man, it was surprising that he should say to him: 'Ah, so you must be Phil's Father?' Paul was naturally delighted to be aged by 25 years at a stroke, which I'm sure did wonders for his confidence just before he was about to do his best man's speech!

The story of Mark Anthony
On the subject of getting names right, a friend of mine, Mark Anthony, kindly told me his own story:

I am, in fact, Mark Anthony III, my father being II and his father I. Given the general confusion that this caused at any family gathering, my family always call me by my second name, Sean. On my wedding day I decided to have my father as my best man. Having never actually spoken publicly before, he was absolutely terrified. Approximately 10 seconds into his speech about me – Sean – and Ruth, one of my new wife's relatives stands up and shouts:

'Who the hell is this Sean bloke? Am I at the right wedding?'

My father quickly went to pieces after that. Although with hindsight, it did prevent him from telling too many embarrassing stories.

Do not embarrass your ex-wife

Just as we find that many people use their wedding speech as an opportunity to show off their, often non-existent, comedic skills, many brides' fathers use their speech as an opportunity to have a go at their ex-wife. I have seen this happen, and however subtly they try to do it, it always falls flat. Your wedding speech is not the time nor the place to do this, and once you have done it, and doubtless failed to achieve the desired result, your speech will not recover. Your wedding speech is a time for celebration, and holding the microphone does not entitle you to hijack the proceedings.

Far better is to always say how proud you are of your daughter, and if you have helpful advice you want to share on the secrets of how to have a happy marriage then let's hear it.

Use of humour

Earlier in this book I said that humour can be both very powerful and indeed potentially very destructive. Do not set out to be funny. A good story told well, will always be just as good as if not better than a straight joke.

QUICK TIP

A particularly good technique is to compare and contrast how you met your own wife, with how your new son-in-law met your daughter. You can compare how you first met your wife, how you got to know each other, where you used to go for entertainment, how and when you first set up home together, and so on. It is surprising how many differences there are between the two generations, and this can be extremely funny when told well.

Look to the future

Just as you have talked about the past, it is also good to look to the future. A wedding is a great opportunity to do this, and it helps guests to imagine and think about what may be in store for the happy couple as the years go by. Again, getting the audience to use their imaginations is a trick used by many professional speakers, and it helps people to remember what you are saying.

FINAL THOUGHTS

The father of the bride has the unenviable responsibility of being on first, warming up the guests by setting the tone and pace for the speeches, welcoming everyone officially and proposing a toast to the health and happiness of the bride and groom.

A tough act to follow by any standard!

10

The Groom

I can't say that my speech at my own wedding was particularly brilliant, as I didn't make one. Lynne said a few words; she started at about 2:10 and went on for – now, how long have we been married?

Anon

We said earlier that it is the job of the groom to do most of the official thanking on the day. In particular, he should thank everyone who has helped with the organisation (and perhaps funding) of the wedding, the bridesmaids, pageboys, ushers and so on, the guests for coming and for their very kind gifts.

It is possible, and boring for everyone else, to thank *too many* people. I have heard all of the following people being thanked by various grooms: dentists, solicitors, employers, bookmakers, bank managers, plumbers (in fact, I called out the plumber on my own wedding day), tailors, independent financial advisers, probation officers, and a groom who once thanked his football team captain for allowing him the weekend off.

ENTERTAINMENT VALUE

As well as thanking everyone, the groom's speech should also have a certain entertainment value, though not to the extent that it becomes a cheap variety act. Some friends told me recently about a wedding they attended where the groom was a motivational speaker. Not surprisingly, there was considerable anticipation of the speech amongst the guests, and true to form, his words weaved, danced and flowed like a true professional. But it was when he likened his bride to a warm, milky drink that it started to go wrong:

Victoria is like a cappuccino – hot, frothy and bubbly on top; dark, strong and bitter underneath.

I think the guests probably knew what he was trying to say, but even if you are a highly experienced speaker, do try to remember that this is a wedding. Don't overcook your speech!

Remember it's not a competition

In terms of its entertainment value, the groom's speech should fall somewhere between that of the bride's father and the best man. In terms of sensitivities, if you are a regular presenter or speaker as part of your work or perhaps a bit of a natural show-off, you might want to consider not showing off or showing up the bride's father. Wedding speeches are supposed to be sincere but entertaining, but not to the extent that it is a competition to be judged by the guests with a 'clap-o-meter'.

I say this because at more than one wedding, I have witnessed speeches where there was clearly rivalry or competition, albeit friendly between the groom and the bride's father. On one such occasion, immediately after the groom's speech, his wife's father leapt to his feet again to say a few more words which he had apparently previously forgotten. Not to be outdone, the groom then said a bit more – only for the bride's father to get up yet again. It was only when the bride and her mother started heckling that the 'rivals' both sat down.

What else should you include?

Your speech is not merely an opportunity *just* to thank people, and personally, I would be inclined to address a good portion of the content of your speech to the bride's father and mother. Remember that your wife's father will (hopefully) have said what a good bloke you are in his speech, and will have ever so subtly told you that he expects you to look after her, for better or for worse, in sickness and in health and so on – you get the picture. A good chunk of your speech should therefore acknowledge your new father-in-law's speech and to take on board the points raised.

QUICK TIP

Even if you have thoroughly prepared and rehearsed your speech, it is absolutely vital that you are prepared to make some off the cuff remarks specifically to your father-in-law and his wife in response to what he has said. Apart from anything else, it is common courtesy.

All good speeches at any occasion, whether business or pleasure, should include a healthy dose of humility and compassion for the listener. Use your speech to prove to your father-in-law (or at least say to him) that you really do care. This is a very big moment for him and his wife, and they will be very appreciative if the person to whom they are handing over their daughter expresses humbleness, caring and sensitivity.

The most entertaining speeches from grooms usually make reference to how he and his bride first met. It never ceases to amaze me how nature and random chance conspire to create a sequence of events which eventually result in a groom telling his and his wife's story at their wedding reception. And, as we say elsewhere in this book, it is this and other stories which will be key to captivating your guests in your speech. Stories about how you both met, how the relationship developed, when you bought your first vacuum cleaner and so on appear to hold endless fascination for the guests – even if they already know the anecdotes. By the telling of the stories, the guests get to see 'behind the scenes' of your relationship, which like all the best TV documentaries, is absolutely fascinating.

QUICK TIP

Mention any friends or relatives who were around at the time or who perhaps engineered the first meeting with your wife. It is entirely reasonable to make humorous remarks or jokes at their expense. They will enjoy having their names mentioned and it will also be entertaining for anyone who knows them.

More often than not, the best man will have been implicated in the plot back when you first met, so it's great to get in a few words about him before he launches into his speech. Whilst you will no doubt be wondering what your best man is going to say about you, it is always a good idea to just check that he is not using any of the same stories as you. You don't want to steal his thunder or he might end up using a story that he was in two minds about and you can bet that it will be the one story that you don't want everyone to hear!

QUICK TIP

A good technique which professional speakers use, is to try to tell self-deprecating stories or those which make light of yourself. This shows a good dose of humility and is particularly entertaining for everyone else.

Equally, try not to get too many laughs at your wife's expense. You might get away with just one – like a characteristic which is common knowledge to everyone – but I have seen some grooms spend almost their entire speech revealing their wife's closest personal secrets or habits. Again, a good dig in the ribs or a swift, sharp kick under the table usually puts a stop to it.

FINAL THOUGHTS

Look to the future, your future happiness, and express how excited you are about enjoying many fantastic years together. Express your undying love directly to your new wife – telling it straight from the heart. Rehearse this bit by all means, but certainly don't read it from your notes. If your wife and your guests can see that you are truly sincere, I can promise that your speech will be a hit.

11

The Best Man

Right at the end, the best man got the bride and groom to stand up and look into each other's eyes, and said: 'Statistically, you are now looking at the person most likely to kill you!'

Dr Andy Pardoe

On paper, this remark looks a little odd to say the least, but apparently it brought the house down. And more often than not, the best man can get away with murder in his speech. In fact sometimes, the guests will be disappointed if there isn't a good dose of quality off-the-wall material.

Generally speaking, the guests are anticipating a good show from the best man, as his speech is often seen as the climax of the wedding speeches. We discovered earlier that the role of the best man is to provide the main act of the proceedings. It is often eagerly awaited by the guests, and nervously anticipated by the groom and his bride.

EMBARRASS BUT DO NOT HUMILIATE THE GROOM!

The contents of the best man's speech should follow a time-honoured formula, which starts with the groom carefully schooling the best man beforehand in what he can and cannot include. Money, favours or beer may even change hands to ensure discretion, prudence and tact, only for the groom to be submitted at the reception to the most brutal of verbal assaults on his honesty, trustworthiness, faithfulness, sexual prowess, sobriety, reliability, commitment – and just about every other aspect of his character. Past employers of the groom offer their comments on the quality of the groom's work and the prospects for his future career (to the obvious horror of the bride's parents), past girlfriends are listed (in order) together with appalling stories of how and why they split up; and stories are recounted of holidays and five-day drinking sessions that resulted in the groom being found naked on Clapham Common . . . with a goat.

There is always an added frisson of excitement to the best man's speech when all the guests know that he used to go out with the bride. His speech then has the potential to go down a road which can only lead to a cliff edge, particularly if the best man has had a couple of drinks beforehand. Drinking and driving towards cliff edges will result in the inevitable, as was the case when such a best man (a contributor to this book who will remain nameless) suggested that the bride had 'been round the block a bit'. Turning to the groom he said:

> You are marrying a girl who is pure and simple – and I should know. Ha ha ha!

Not surprisingly, the groom, the bride and their families have never spoken to him since.

Whilst this can be extremely funny and embarrassing for the guests, it has the potential to upset a few people – not least of whom will be the bride and her parents. Care, discretion and good judgement do need to be exercised, though it never ceases to amaze me how many best men will let rip with both barrels with little care for sensitivities and decency. Long friendships between grooms and their best men have been known to end abruptly at weddings, solely because the latter went a bit over the top.

The best man's speech should not be dedicated entirely to trawling through the groom's unspeakable past, comical and side-splitting as it may be. As a close friend of the groom, you will presumably have a strong bond of friendship and respect perhaps going back a great many years. This is your opportunity to show your admiration and high regard for your friend and to express sincerely what a genuinely decent guy he is.

Balance the unspeakable with the speakable, recalling stories and anecdotes of positive things the groom has done or achieved. Remember that approximately half of the guests will not know him, and they undoubtedly would like to discover something of the merits and qualities of this fine man.

QUICK TIP

By all means mention past girlfriends, but put this into context and perhaps describe how the groom was smitten instantly when he met the (now) bride. Describe how they met, how the relationship developed and provide an insight into how this day has come about.

MESSAGES FROM THOSE UNABLE TO ATTEND

Another key job is to read out any last minute messages – letters, postcards, emails, email greetings cards and, not surprisingly, text messages.

I have seen a number of best men make the most of this splendid duty by adding a modern touch to the proceedings, and formally, if not rather theatrically, switching on their mobile phone in front of the guests. Holding their Nokia aloft they announce like a TV game show host: 'Let's see who has sent a text . . .'. They are rewarded just moments later by a loud 'beep, beep, beep' as the texts arrive through the ether and are greeted by a rapturous cheer from the guests.

QUICK TIP

A word of advice here to any best men who would like to try this – just make absolutely sure that someone has actually sent a text beforehand, otherwise this will fall a little flat! And don't be tempted to check beforehand that the texts have arrived, or you will miss out on getting the full effect of the 'beep, beep, beep'. It makes all the difference!

MAKING THE TOAST

Apart from reading out messages of congratulations, the best man does have a few other formal duties to perform, including responding on behalf of the 'helpers team' such as the bridesmaids, pageboys and ushers, and proposing a toast to the bride and groom. If you *have* gone a little over the top with risqué material, the toast to the happy couple is your last chance to redeem yourself, and trust me you will if you are sincere! Make your toast deep, heartfelt and meaningful, by really putting in the effort to make it an exciting final flourish in your speech.

QUICK TIP

If you have room, take a step forward as you start the toast, stand up straight, look around the room at as many guests as possible, pause, take a deep breath and project your voice – speaking with authority and passion. If you only have time to rehearse one bit of your speech, then make it this part. As you say the final words 'to the bride and groom', look them in the eye, smile at them broadly making sure they can see that you mean it.

If you have used the services of a master of ceremonies or a toastmaster, take careful note of how they address the guests and try to emulate their style and approach.

FINAL THOUGHTS

In conclusion, the best man's speech is not just about embarrassing the groom and telling funny stories. It's also about showing real sincerity – a quality most admired in the best speakers.

(12)

The Mother of the Bride and the Mother of the Groom

There is little in wedding tradition that says the mothers of the bride or groom should make a speech – though increasingly you will see mums leaping to their feet in answer to the chant: 'Speech, speech!' The mums' speeches are still relatively uncommon, but an impromptu speech or a few words may be said at some point in the proceedings.

However, there will be situations when either of the mothers will make a more formal speech, and these may include:

◆ When the bride's father has died or is unable to attend for other reasons such as illness, work, prison and so on.

◆ When there has been a recent family bereavement and there is a desire for someone other than the main participants to pay tribute.

◆ When friends or relatives have travelled a very long distance to attend.

◆ When friends or relatives have not been seen for many years.

◆ When special thanks need to be made to a particular individual for their help with perhaps the organisation or funding of the wedding.

◆ When the bride, groom or another member of the family has experienced trauma, tragedy or endured particular hardship or suffering at some point in their lives.

MOTHERS' IMPROMPTU SPEECHES

These are not the only reasons why either of the mothers would wish to say a few words, but they are often the catalyst. More often than not, however, the mothers will speak as a response to the guests calling for them to say something, or they want to make 'thank yous' or indeed feel a sudden urge to get to their feet. It happens!

There aren't any particular things that *have* to be said or people who have to be thanked or toasted. The mothers' speeches usually come from a spontaneous desire to express health, wealth and happiness to their much loved offspring. Such speeches can often be very moving and universally praised and applauded by the guests.

As you will already have gathered, I am an advocate of thorough preparation for your wedding speech, but very often improvised speeches can in fact be outstanding. It is their very spontaneous, spur-of-the-moment nature which makes them work – as more often than not, the words come very much from the heart. Again, as we said earlier, sincerity is a key ingredient of any speech or presentation, and this comes across very strongly when the heart rules the head.

There is of course a difference between unrehearsed and impromptu, so don't fall into the trap of believing that you don't need to think about what you are going to say if you are planning to say something. If you intend to speak, then plan it and practise it, perhaps getting help and advice from someone else. Make a point of checking to see if the other mother intends to speak, and make sure that you aren't both intending to say exactly the same thing.

DO THE MOTHERS NEED ANY PARTICULAR SPEAKING SKILLS?

No more than anyone else making a speech. From experience, the ladies tend to be a little softer spoken, and the guests seem to have a bit more respect for them than for the men – often staying very hushed so that everything can be heard. I have also found that the guests appear slightly more attentive to the mothers and this can only be a good thing.

> **QUICK TIP**
>
> If there is an option of using a microphone, then take it up.

However strong the urge was to say something, most mothers tell me that they were extremely nervous and admit to shaking like leaves for about an hour after their big moment. Female speakers also appear to have better eye contact with guests, and their thanks to various people comes across as very sincere.

Finally, there is absolutely no need to try to be funny. The mothers often decide to speak because they have something to say or a story to tell. As I have said earlier, a message or story told well will always come across more effectively than a poorly told or unrehearsed joke. Mind you, on one occasion I saw the groom's mother pretend to tell him off over some misdemeanour that occurred twelve years previously, which he didn't think she was aware of. This went down very well with the guests. To his horror, she even pretended to smack his backside!

QUICK TIP

My one constructive piece of advice to the mothers is to smile a bit more during the speech. Of the mothers' speeches that I have seen, they can sometimes appear a little serious, but can easily be lifted with a cheery smile.

WHEN MIGHT THE MOTHERS SPEAK?

Again, there are no hard and fast rules. Unless they are making a speech for one of the reasons at the start of this chapter, their speeches are very often a bit of an afterthought and usually make a surprise appearance after the best man's speech. And sometimes, the mothers are able to beautifully take the wind out of the best man's sails by making a skilful and witty reference to his speech. For example:

Thank you to young James – I enjoyed every week of that wonderful introduction to my own speech.

Guaranteed to get a big laugh and to get the guests on to your side.

FINAL THOUGHTS

Almost without exception, all of the mothers' speeches that I've heard have been excellent. A little short maybe, but all the better for it. I hope that such speeches will, in time, become part of wedding tradition.

(13)

The Bride

At most wedding receptions, it comes as a very pleasant surprise to everyone if the bride makes a speech. Again, it is not traditional for her to do so, but the custom is growing in popularity and is more commonplace than speeches from the mothers of the bride and groom or sundry uncles that would 'like a turn'! It's worth bearing in mind that at least half of the guests will know the bride, and would naturally enjoy hearing what she has to say.

WHEN SHOULD THE BRIDE SPEAK?

Some people say that the bride should speak after the groom and before the best man. However, there really is no hard and fast rule, but like the mothers' speeches, the bride's tends to come last. This does take a bit of the edge off the best man's speech, but hey, this is the bride's day after all – she can speak whenever she wants to!

On the occasions when I have heard a bride speak, most speeches were made on the spur of the moment in response to a rowdy section of guests calling out for her to do so, or when she suddenly remembered that she wanted to thank a few people.

However, there might be occasions when a bride decides in

advance of the wedding that she would like to speak and these could include:

◆ When her father, mother or a very close member of the family is unable to attend.

◆ There has been a recent bereavement, illness, tragedy or problem in the family that has touched or affected everyone.

◆ To announce something very special, positive or exciting that has happened in the family, such as a recent birth, another marriage or maybe a success or celebration.

◆ There is a particularly strong bond between the bride and a parent or step-parent.

◆ A significant proportion of the guests is made up of the bride's work colleagues or friends.

◆ A long lost relative or friend has travelled a very long distance to attend.

◆ The bride would like to make a point of formally thanking someone for a kindness done to the family or perhaps for help with the wedding arrangements that went beyond the call of duty.

Either way, whilst it is not fixed into tradition for the bride to speak, increasingly the guests demand that she does! It is as well to be ready for this to happen and to prepare something, however short, so that you can respond relatively confidently. This way, you can make what *looks* like an impromptu speech, but which has actually been prepared in advance – a mark of all great speakers!

A LITTLE PREPARATION GOES A LONG WAY

As the bride, your preparation really does not need to be any more than just jotting down a few notes about *who* you would like to mention or thank and *why*. Potentially this can give you a 20-minute speech without really trying. I'm not saying that you *should* speak for that long, but go for it by all means if that's what you want to do. The bride is about the only person who can get away with going on a bit too long, so why not make the most of your time in the limelight?

When I have heard a bride go on for too long, it has never felt that way, but I did once hear someone go through a list of just about anyone she had ever met. She did it with a broad grin on her face and everyone loved it – at least until her boss threw a bread roll at her! Most of the brides I've heard speak have been on their feet for anything between one and five minutes.

WHAT SHOULD THE BRIDE SAY?

There are some people you really do need to mention, such as your parents, your maid or matron of honour (if you have one), your bridesmaids and your pageboys – even if they have already been thanked by everyone else. In addition to thanking people, you could say a few words *about* them – perhaps something that other guests don't know about them but would find interesting or surprising to learn. Of course, there's also your husband whom you might want to talk about as well. You could talk about how you met your husband, and what your first thoughts were about him and his friends.

If you are speaking after your husband and he has already described how you both met, you might like to tell the same story, but from your own perspective. Often the story is told very differently and this usually goes down very well with the guests.

Talking about your husband's friends is also a good move because first, people like to hear their name mentioned, and second, it will endear you to them and your husband's friends and family. A good idea is to make a point of highlighting a couple of his friends, perhaps recounting a story about them which reflects their characters, personalities or temperaments. A story about when you first met them and what you thought about them is virtually guaranteed to get some laughs. Your husband will also enjoy it.

FINAL THOUGHTS

In conclusion, the bride's speech is almost always universally enjoyed by all the guests, family and friends. In some respects it is surprising that it has not been a tradition for her to speak, but it is great that more and more brides are leaping boldly to their feet – whether on the spur of the moment when egged on by others or when planned carefully in advance.

If you are reading this book as a bride-to-be, my advice is to go for it anyway – don't wait to be pushed into it by your relatives, friends and work colleagues. Any worries, nerves or concerns that you have now or on the big day will quickly disappear and I promise you will end up thoroughly enjoying yourself. And by making a speech of your own, you are guaranteed to add another fantastic memory to your very special day.

14

Speaking Tips for Different Character Types

As was mentioned in the Preface, no two people are the same. That is one of the most appealing things about listening to great speeches as you get to hear and experience a whole variety of different character types and personalities. You hear people from different social backgrounds, countries and cultures and discover something of their lives. Whatever type of speech that you are listening to, whether a business speech, a motivational speech or a wedding speech, it is often the characters of the speakers and the stories they tell that bring their speeches to life.

And different people tell their stories in different ways, because some of us are shy, some of us are confident, some of us are nervous, some of us are funny and some of us are more serious. Either way, we need to know how to get our message across to the audience or guests in a way which complements our character and personality.

From experience of listening to a multitude of different people at different weddings, I have included some tips for the three main character types I have seen sometimes struggle with their speeches. As you will discover, it is not just shy or nervous people who can sometimes find their speech a challenge. Even confident people have problems. These tips apply equally to everyone.

TIPS FOR VERY SHY PEOPLE

Keep it short and sincere

'Keep it short' will be welcome advice to shy people. Public speaking is not everyone's idea of fun and it is even less so for those who are very shy. But the answer is really simple. It is *not* compulsory for you to lecture the guests for the best part of an hour and the guests will in fact thank you for your brevity. For starters, people who know you may already realise that you are a little shy and will have made allowances for that. Weddings are generally very good-humoured affairs and it is most unlikely that you will be booed off stage. Trust me on this.

The solution is to decide in advance what it is that you *want* to say. There will always be something. Provided you say it with sincerity, that is all that matters. I repeat – provided you say it with sincerity, that is all that matters.

Don't *try* to be funny

There is a common misconception that wedding speeches have to be funny and that the guests are required to roll around the floor in hysterics. Not so.

I have said elsewhere in this book that you don't need to try to be funny by including jokes. Far better is to include stories or anecdotes. In short, if you are shy, or do not believe you are funny, then don't try to be just because you think it's the thing to do as part of a wedding speech.

I do not believe myself to be very good at telling jokes. For one thing I can never remember them anyway and am always in awe of people who can reel off dozens one after the other. I have about two really rude jokes that I *can* remember, neither of which would be particularly appropriate for a wedding! But I do think I can tell a good story and after I have told it a few times, for some reason audiences find it funnier and funnier. I guess this tells me that practice is important – both in getting the words right and in the delivery. For example, I have learnt when to pause at certain parts of the story, where I should look and so on and the more I work on these small points, the better the delivery.

QUICK TIP

Don't feel you need to tell jokes or to be consciously funny. Just concentrate on what you do want to say, and if you can embellish it with a story or two, so much the better.

Smile

Whether you are an experienced or inexperienced speaker, shy or confident, smiling is one of the most powerful tricks of the trade. A smile is infectious – just as a frown, scowl or grimace is off-putting. And even if you are the shyest person in the world, you can still manage a smile – however brief.

QUICK TIP

Smile right at the start of your speech, and try to do it again regularly throughout. If you have to write it into your notes to remind you, then do so.

You may not believe it, but many top professional speakers write 'SMILE!' at strategic points in their notes. And yes, smile again at the end of your speech – the guests will love it, and guess what, it will make you feel happier in yourself.

Have a glass of champagne

Many professional speakers advocate that you don't touch alcohol before a speech. And that's fair enough, but this is a wedding after all, and it would be churlish to suggest rather pompously that you shouldn't touch a drop of the hard stuff before your big moment.

If you are quite shy, then there is certainly no harm in having a glass to help boost your confidence. Champagne is ideal because it is not too bulky (like a pint of bitter) and not too strong. The fresh taste and the bubbles will certainly perk you up. However, remember *only* a glass or two (see my notes in Chapter 4 on alcohol consumption at weddings).

Express affection

I have found in the past that people who are a little shy are often able to articulate their affection and expressions of thanks very well. Their words are often more carefully thought-through and they have the ability to express what they mean in a clearer fashion than some more confident people.

This is a useful skill to have and it is a good idea to make the most of this strength in your wedding speech. This means it is worth concentrating the contents of your speech on saying what people (family, friends, specific guests) mean to you and how much you care for them.

Look at someone you know well

If you are shy, it is always helpful to have strong moral support, so try to find someone amongst the guests whom you know well, and occasionally look at them during your speech.

QUICK TIP

You may want to tell them in advance that you are going to do this now and again and why. When you do look at them, you are likely to be met with a wink or smile to help boost your confidence.

Use notes

Whilst the best and most engaging speeches tend to come from speakers who are not using notes, some very shy people will feel more confident if they have something to refer to. This is not because they are more likely to forget their speech (I have seen no evidence to suggest this happens), but because the notes or cards provide a base point which acts as a sort of comfort zone.

Apart from anything else, the use of notes will help to boost your confidence and self-assurance. I do not really advocate reading a script in full unless you are experienced in reading aloud, but short notes or keywords are very helpful.

Don't look down

Some shy people have a tendency to look down as they speak, either in conversation or in a presentation. This is not generally conducive to clear communication and has the added effect of making you *look* shy. It also points the direction of your voice downwards, which can make it difficult for people to hear what you are saying.

It is entirely possible to make a speech as a shy person without appearing shy but if you do tend to look down, you will look shy and potentially influence the guests' perceptions of you.

I mentioned earlier that it is a good idea to find a friend in the audience and to look at them from time to time. This helps to stop you looking down, so you might want to find two or three others to pick on as well. This should not prove too difficult, because if you are speaking at a wedding, the chances are you will know quite a few people.

> **QUICK TIP**
>
> If you have difficulty looking people in the eye, then perhaps look to the back of the room, or spots such as pictures or light fittings on the wall.

Practise reading out loud

Reading out loud is a huge confidence-builder and is easy to do. I am always banging on about the importance of rehearsing your speech, but many people find this difficult – even when they are on their own.

First of all, you need to know your material and then you need to work on the delivery. But if you are not the most confident of people, even speaking out loud to yourself in the privacy of your own car, bathroom or bedroom can still be quite difficult. So practise, practise, practise and your confidence will gradually improve every day.

When I was about 11 years old, I was asked to read the lesson at the school carol service. To practise, my mother made me read the lesson out loud at the top of our very long Victorian staircase as she and our cat looked up from below.

> And there were in the same country shepherds abiding in the field . . .

The words of the Gospel according to St Luke were clearly lost on the cat, but the combination of the height and distance was strangely empowering and made me feel enormously confident. Reading the words out loud 25 times made me very familiar with the material, and got me used to speaking out loud and projecting my voice.

When it came to the big day at the church, it was a doddle. There was also an unexpected benefit – I realised that I knew the words almost by heart, and so I was able to spend more time speaking to the congregation rather than reading my notes.

Practise your speech
Having read the above, it follows that practice is very important. If nothing else, it builds your confidence – something that will be extremely helpful if you are shy, withdrawn or lack confidence.

Don't fiddle!

I don't really understand the psychology as to why this happens, but some speakers who lack confidence tend to fiddle. In fact, speakers who are confident fiddle as well! People will fiddle with their fingers, their (new) wedding ring, their notes, their wine glass, their cutlery – anything they can lay their hands on.

Whilst this is hardly the end of the world, it is noticed by the audience or guests and adds to the perception that you are shy or nervous. I appreciate that you have quite enough to think about, but try to control yourself!

In fact, it doesn't really matter if you put one hand in your pocket with the other holding your notes. Presentation skills training regrettably still concentrates a lot on the importance of having your tie straight, shiny shoes, not jangling change in your pocket and so on. And this is a shame, because these points are not really the important things to consider.

Many speakers for example quite deliberately hold something as a prop, such as their spectacles or a pointer. My wife describes this as a 'psychological crutch' – the speaking equivalent of worry beads. Apparently, I held a glass of champagne throughout my wedding speech and occasionally sipped from it, which probably explains a lot!

QUICK TIP

If you are going to hold on to something during your speech, use it creatively or to enhance your performance – but *don't* fiddle with it!

Visualise everyone smiling

I have talked about visualisation techniques elsewhere in this book, but they are worth repeating here. Visualisation is an extremely powerful technique which will help people who are shy or lack confidence.

The trick behind visualisation is that you get to 'see' the desired result or outcome before the event. By picturing in your imagination precisely how you want the guests to respond you are tricking your subconscious into believing that it is real. If you spend time seeing yourself speaking and feeling confident, with the guests smiling broadly and enjoying themselves, when the big day arrives, you will have already predetermined what will happen.

This is a technique which really does work, and with practice, you will be amazed at how effective it can be in improving your confidence – not only when speaking, but in life generally.

TIPS FOR VERY CONFIDENT PEOPLE

We would all like to be supremely confident when making a speech of any description. Unfortunately, this attribute of our character does not necessarily add to our conviction or the clarity of our speech, and being a naturally confident person does not mean that you will not experience nerves before making a speech. Sometimes the combination of confidence and nerves combines to produce a heady cocktail resulting in nothing short of fireworks! Here are some tips to – hopefully – keep you on your best behaviour.

Speak slowly

It is all too easy to become carried away with the excitement of the situation, or the opportunity to grab the limelight, but equally this confidence can cause more problems than you can imagine.

Not least of which is the tendency to gabble on or speak too fast, thus rendering your speech completely incomprehensible. For the guests, this can be disappointing. They know that you are a confident and outgoing individual, but it can be a let down when they have to sit or stand through a speech that is jumbled, incoherent, disjointed, confused and unintelligible – sorry!

QUICK TIP

Try to make the most of your confidence by consciously slowing yourself down and channelling your self-assurance into getting your message across with clarity and conviction.

Keep it short – don't ramble on and on and on

Another characteristic of very confident people is a tendency sometimes to go on a bit too long. The sound of their own voice can be irresistible, and given a stage and a microphone, the inevitable happens!

There is an old adage that says 'less is more' and it certainly applies to weddings – your speech is not supposed to be a platform for ruthless self-promotion.

QUICK TIP

When preparing your speech, write down everything that you think you will want to say and then cut out more than you feel comfortable with. This should leave just the really good stuff, which you can then deliver in your own inimitable style.

Keep it short – ideally leave the guests wanting more.

Don't have too much to drink

In Chapter 4 I mentioned the importance of not having too much to drink. Weddings are very relaxed and happy occasions which often extend over many hours. It can be all too easy to have a lot to drink before the speeches start, and different character types may be more inclined to imbibe much more than others amid the general bonhomie of the occasion. I have seen this happen several times, when some of the more socially outgoing and self-assured wedding participants get carried away with the excitement of the day, and end up extremely tired (as a newt).

If you have to make a speech, tread carefully when you are near the bar.

Be sincere

Much as we mentioned in Keep it Short above, the naturally confident individual can occasionally get carried away during their speech. If you possess such confidence, it is important to restrain that attribute and to use it sparingly.

Natural exuberance, energy and enthusiasm is an attractive characteristic, but can sometimes come across in speeches as being slightly cocky, arrogant or brash, leaving many of the guests questioning your sincerity. With care and control of your natural optimism, confidence and high spirits you will be able to leave the guests in no doubt as to your sincerity.

Don't mention too many people no one knows

One of my pet irritants at weddings or in clubs and societies is how speakers often rabbit on about people or individuals that no one else knows. Whilst this makes those 'in the know' feel more part of a clique, it goes straight over the heads of everyone else – to the point that it can be annoying for them.

Many naturally confident people have a wide circle of friends and are often at the centre of things. However, just as we do not want the father of the bride to list out all his daughter's class friends or GCSE grades, we do not want any speaker to talk too much about their huge group of friends that no one else knows. I have said previously in this book that it is good to mention some of the guests by name as it helps them to feel included and valued as friends. But my advice is try to make sure that the people you mention are actually present and that you do not make too many comments that others would regard as 'in jokes'. The idea of mentioning people is to make them feel involved, but overstep the mark and others will feel excluded.

Don't shout

I have a good friend who shall remain nameless. He is energetic, enthusiastic, positive, optimistic, full of life – and loud! Everyone likes him and he is the life and soul of the party. But to some people, loudness can be very off-putting, particularly so in a speech.

Voice and speech coaches will tell you that projecting your voice is not about shouting – but that is precisely what some very confident people do during their wedding speech! Most people are suitably nervous before their speech, which has the effect of quietening them down a bit, but nerves can make confident, self-assured people go in exactly the opposite direction and end up bellowing at the guests. Be warned!

Don't talk about yourself

One of the most refreshing points about a wedding speech is that, unlike many business speeches or presentations, it should not be about the speaker. Talking about yourself is a classic trap which many confident speakers fall into and is desperately dull at the best of times, let alone during a wedding speech.

Just about the only person who can get away with talking about themselves is the bride. The bride's father can also do it to a certain extent when he says how proud he and his wife feel.

> **QUICK TIP**
>
> If you are a confident individual, use that natural ability to your advantage and talk about anything but yourself!

Watch your step!

Sometimes each of us looks at confident people and wishes we were like them – outgoing, positive, forthright and so on. But certainly in terms of making a speech, these characteristics are not always helpful.

I have seen some such people get so involved in their speech that it becomes more like the performance of a motivational speaker who prowls and leaps across the stage. And just as we have seen countless people fall over on television out-take programmes, so have I seen people fall over during their wedding speech.

I witnessed one bride get an accidental cut to the chin as her husband animatedly made a point about football (yes, football again) – punching the air as he likened the first meeting with his (now) wife with the scoring of a goal.

Take care with your enthusiasm and confidence – it can be dangerous!

TIPS FOR VERY NERVOUS PEOPLE

Some people *just know* that they are going to be nervous before their speech and can feel the 'butterflies' building some weeks before the big day. Others only feel the nerves kick in about an hour or so beforehand. Either way, for most people it is not a very pleasant experience, and I don't actually think it is possible to completely remove the feeling of nerves altogether. So here are some tips to help if you are one of those people who really does not care for public speaking, but are ready and willing.

One drink only

Here I would give much the same advice as I did for shy people. Your speech is not a business presentation where your every word and movement will be scrutinised for clues as to the quality and excellence of your company. This is a wedding speech and so should be put firmly in the fun category of presentations.

By all means, have a drink to give yourself Dutch courage, but for goodness sake, don't overdo it! Have no more than will just loosen you up a bit – and even then try not to drink on an empty stomach.

Alcohol is not always the answer – water can be just as effective and has the added benefit of oiling your throat.

Deep breaths

Over the years I have read much about the importance of deep breathing to ease the nerves before a speech. I have also attended some excellent presentation skills courses where you are taught how to breathe properly in order to project yourself clearly and to reduce stress on your voice.

Regular speakers will know how off-putting it can be to feel your voice tensing up, and this can have the effect of throwing you off your stride. So if you are able to control your breathing, there are a number of benefits.

QUICK TIP

Take long, deep breaths for a couple of minutes before the speech, if only to get you breathing in a regular pattern. Nerves can shorten your breath which is not conducive to making you feel calm. I was always told to concentrate on the exhale and to breathe out as slowly as possible – there is no doubt that this helped.

Smile and laugh

Again, similar advice as for shy people – smiling broadly and laughing with friends is a great way of easing tension. It is a conduit for releasing your pent-up nerves and really helps to make you feel more relaxed.

One of the main reasons why people feel nervous is because they are focusing on themselves and how they think people will respond to them. My advice is to switch your energies away from focusing on yourself and your speech, and on to the guests and their enjoyment.

A similar thing happens when people make business presentations. Most presenters are so focused on their laptop and whether the technology will work, that they forget to focus on the audience. In short – too much inward focused attention actually makes you *more* stressed, so change your focus to the guests and to connecting with them by smiling and laughing with them.

Rehearse

The importance of rehearsal has been mentioned several times in this book – and rightly so, so I don't intend to repeat too much of it again here.

In short, the nervous speaker will discover that there is no single better way of easing their nerves than to know what they are talking about or to have been through what they are going to talk about several times.

Rehearsals give you confidence – pure and simple.

Use of notes

Using notes, perhaps in the form of cue cards, can also help if you are feeling very nervous. They are not, however, a replacement for proper rehearsal time, but they can and will make you feel more confident (see Chapter 8 for more on using notes).

Tell people that you are nervous

Whilst I am not an advocate of saying 'I'll tell you now that I'm pretty rubbish at public speaking', which doesn't quite set the right tone, I *do* think it is OK to tell people that you are nervous. People will have guessed as much anyway, but on the occasions that I have seen speakers start off their talk with this admission, it is usually received very well. Humility is always a good attribute in any speaker.

Oh, what the hell – here goes

Just go for it!

Diving in at the deep end is one of the best ways of getting over your nerves. Most speakers are quite surprised at how quickly the nerves disappear once they start their speech, and are ready to do it again as soon as they sit down – a bit like doing a parachute jump. Yes, they are shaking like a leaf afterwards, but it feels more like an adrenaline rush than the awful sick feeling that accompanies pre-speech nerves.

Any kind of public speaking practice will help enormously, or get in touch with a professional presentation skills coach who will be able to help. Like all things in life, once you have given something a go, it generally becomes very much easier than you were expecting.

And, as we have said above, it is not as though your liberty depends on your speech. You are generally amongst friends!

FINAL THOUGHTS

I hope that some of these tips will be helpful to you. They reflect the problems that are most likely to be encountered by a wide range of different people. If you have any particular issues or problems, feel free to email us at enquiries@greatweddingspeech.com.

If there is one tip I can give you that will help above all else it would be – yes, you've guessed it – rehearse!

(15)

Using Ready-made Material

You will have discovered by now that one of the main premises of this book is that your wedding speech should come from the heart. It should be your own.

Why? Those speeches that do come from the heart are invariably better received by the guests. Sincerity is everything – and it shows. Your speech isn't something that you can write in a rush, print and stuff into your jacket pocket. That's why you won't find this book stuffed with jokes, funny one-liners and ready-made speeches. If that's what you want, there are plenty of places you can find them.

For example, my last search on Google under 'wedding speeches' revealed 199,000 pages of resources. Every imaginable wedding situation is covered, with even special sites for people getting hitched for the second time round, and a 5-minute 'crash course' on how to make either the 'ultimate' or better still, the 'perfect' wedding speech. There's even a website with a 'wedding speech wizard'. It asks you a few questions, you click a button, and out comes your speech! There's another site where you search through up to 2,000 speeches, and download the one nearest to your requirements. As the site promises: 'With just a few tweaks, you can customise it to your exact requirements.'

One of my favourites is a website which is dedicated to the best man's speech. It has reviewed over 10,000 wedding speeches 'collected from wedding venues everywhere'. I would love to know how they do this – do they have spies or 'plants' all over the world hastily scribbling down or secretly recording our speeches and best jokes? Are bar staff and masters of ceremonies at hotels up and down the land clandestinely moonlighting for the website, quietly going about their double life surreptitiously gathering evidence? Either way, the site is amazing in its detail and contains several one-liners for every possible aspect of a wedding, including opening lines, ice-breakers, the best man's relationship to the groom and observations on *everything* – the ceremony, the reception, the marquee, the pageboys, bridesmaids, the parents, the presents, the stag party and much more. There are also closing thoughts, a selection of toasts and even contingency lines in the event of something going wrong!

A really neat feature is a handy tool with five drop-down boxes covering the groom's character traits, his interests, his past, his career and his appearance. Simply click on each of them in turn and you can find a one-liner to suit the peculiarity you want to highlight. So for example, under 'character traits', there are 53 to choose from. Here are just some of them:

accident-prone, ambitious, arrogant, bad dancer, bad driver, bad cook, couch potato, crooked (!), entrepreneur, extravagant, gullible, heavy drinker, indecisive, lazy, musical, scrounger, sporty, talkative, undomesticated, unreliable, womaniser . . .

By clicking on 'undomesticated', a further 18 lines appear, which you can just slip into your speech. And for those looking for that 'killer line', there is the 'Line of the Month' feature. Full access to the site is available for a snip at £10.

Yet another website will tell you how to get that so important standing ovation from your wedding speech, simply by purchasing their downloadable e-book – one section of which gives you toasts that will have your guests 'crying in their beer'.

With all these wonderful wedding websites out there, they should provide internet access at every hotel or as part of your marquee package, so that you can arrive from the church or register office, log on and download your speech! Simple and very effective . . .

. . . but cheating!

I hope this book is a few steps beyond all that. Yes, our lives are terribly busy these days and it's difficult to find the time to sit down and write a speech – or maybe we just can't be bothered? But I have no doubt in my mind that those who do make the effort will be rewarded. In fact, it will be the guests who will be rewarded the most.

However, using ready-made speeches is not the same thing as making reference to well-known (and some less well-known) extracts from love poems, sonnets, quotes or other passages. I don't have any objection to the use of a maximum of two well chosen and relevant quotations. If they come from someone well-known, it tends to give the quote an added air of authenticity and authority. It also makes it look as though you are either very well read or have made the effort to do some research.

Using short excerpts from famous letters, poems or sonnets is most effective if the quote that you use comes from someone with whom you might have a tentative link – either personally or through your occupation. For example, if you are the groom and you work in IT, you might want to make reference to something that Bill Gates once said:

> In my parents I saw a model where they were really always communicating, doing things together. They were really kind of a team. I wanted some of that magic myself.

If, perhaps you are a financial adviser, you may wish to refer to the words of Willard Scott who said:

> A good marriage is like an incredible retirement fund. You put everything you have into it during your productive life, and over the years it turns from silver to gold to platinum.

I'm not advocating that you say the line as though you made it up yourself. As you say the line, you should acknowledge the author and say what it means to you or use it within the context of what you are saying. For example:

As my hero and mentor Bill Gates once said about marriage: 'In my parents I saw a model where they were really always communicating, doing things together. They were really kind of a team. I wanted some of that magic myself.'

I want to take the opportunity today to pay tribute to my own parents who are celebrating 30 magical years of marriage this year. Trust me – with a tearaway son like me, they needed to work as a team!

On the pages that follow are several more wonderful quotations, which with care and a suitable credit, you may wish to include in your speech. But as a word of advice, don't overdo it. As I said earlier, stick to just one or maybe two really good ones, or they will have exactly the opposite effect from that which you are trying to achieve. Overuse will make you look insincere, which is not exactly what you are aiming for. And even though these are quotations, which by definition can imply that you may read them out loud from your notes or script, does not mean that you should not rehearse their delivery. More than ever, you should practise reading your quotations out loud and not be afraid to put in some proper effort! The original lines were written or said with feeling, so it's important that you try to get that across in your delivery.

My advice is to learn them by heart and to deliver them with passion and conviction. If you get it right, I promise you will bring a tear to the eye of many guests – and yes – you may even get that standing ovation!

SOME USEFUL QUOTATIONS

Martin Luther – There is no more lovely, friendly and charming relationship, communion or company than a good marriage.

Benjamin Franklin – Marriage is the most natural state of man, and the state in which you will find solid happiness.

André Maurois – Marriage is an edifice that must be rebuilt every day.

Chinese proverb – Married couples who love each other tell each other a thousand things without talking.

Harold Nicolson – The great secret of a successful marriage is to treat all disasters as incidents and none of the incidents as disasters.

Marnie Reed Crowell – To keep the fire burning brightly there's one easy rule: keep the two logs together, near enough to keep each other warm and far enough apart – about a finger's breadth – for breathing room. Good fire, good marriage, same rule.

Heinrich Heine – Here's to matrimony, the high sea for which no compass has yet been invented.

Robert C. Dodds – The goal in marriage is not to think alike, but to think together.

Winston Churchill – My most brilliant achievement was my ability to be able to persuade my wife to marry me.

Friedrich Wilhelm Nietzsche – It is not a lack of love, but a lack of friendship that makes unhappy marriages.

Anon – You don't marry someone you can live with, you marry the person who you cannot live without.

Nigerian proverb – Hold a true friend with both your hands.

Barbara Johnson – Never let a problem to be solved become more important than a person to be loved.

Elizabeth Ashley – In a great romance, each person plays a part the other really likes.

James Roosevelt – My father gave me these hints on speech-making: Be sincere, be brief, be seated.

Mark Twain – Eloquence is the essential thing in a speech, not information.

Winston Churchill – There are two things that are more difficult than making an after-dinner speech: Climbing a wall which is leaning toward you and kissing a girl who is leaning away from you.

Mark Twain – It usually takes more than three weeks to prepare a good impromptu speech.

Traditional Irish Blessing
May the road rise to meet you,
May the wind always be at your back,
May the sun shine warm upon your face;
The rains fall soft upon your fields and until we meet again,
May God hold you in the palm of His hand.

J. Willard Marriott – Good timber does not grow with ease; the stronger the wind, the stronger the trees.

Thomas Mann – We don't love qualities, we love persons; sometimes by reason of their defects as well as of their qualities.

Oscar Wilde – Laughter is not at all a bad beginning for a friendship, and it is far the best ending for one.

Kahlil Gibran – Tenderness and kindness are not signs of weakness and despair, but manifestations of strength and resolution.

Saint Basil the Great – A tree is known by its fruit; a man by his deeds. A good deed is never lost; he who sows courtesy reaps friendship, and he who plants kindness gathers love.

David Viscott – To love and be loved is to feel the sun from both sides.

Willa Cather – Where there is great love, there are always miracles.

John Lennon – We've got this gift of love, but love is like a precious plant. You just can't accept it and leave in the cupboard or just think it's going to get on by itself. You've got to keep watering it, really look after it and nurture it.

Katharine Hepburn – Love has nothing to do with what you are expecting to get – only with what you are expecting to give – which is everything.

Ursula LeGuin – Love doesn't just sit there, like a stone; it has to be made, like bread, remade all the time, made new.

Barnett Brickner – Success in marriage does not come merely through finding the right mate, but through being the right mate.

George Levinger – What counts in making a happy marriage is not so much how compatible you are, but how you deal with incompatibility.

Henry Louis Mencken – For it is mutual trust, even more than mutual interest that holds human associations together. Our friends seldom profit us but they make us feel safe . . . Marriage is a scheme to accomplish exactly that same end.

Simone Signoret – Chains do not hold a marriage together. It is threads, hundreds of tiny threads, which sew people together through the years.

Sydney Smith – Marriage resembles a pair of shears, so joined that they cannot be separated; often moving in opposite directions, yet always punishing anyone who comes between them.

Mignon McLaughlin – A successful marriage requires falling in love many times, always with the same person.

Mel Gibson – I think I've scratched the surface after 20 years of marriage. Women want chocolate and conversation.

John Lennon – Everything is clearer when you're in love.

John Lennon – Love is a promise, love is a souvenir, once given never forgotten, never let it disappear.

Erica Jong – Do you want me to tell you something really subversive? Love is everything it's cracked up to be. That's why people are so cynical about it. . . . It really is worth fighting for, being brave for, risking everything for. And the trouble is, if you don't risk anything, you risk even more.

John Lyly – Marriages are made in heaven and consummated on Earth.

Erich Segal – True love comes quietly, without banners or flashing lights. If you hear bells, get your ears checked.

Hannah More – Love never reasons, but profusely gives; gives, like a thoughtless prodigal, its all, and trembles then lest it has done too little.

Johann Wolfgang von Goethe – A life without love, without the presence of the beloved, is nothing but a mere magic-lantern show. We draw out slide after slide, swiftly tiring of each, and pushing it back to make haste for the next.

George Sand – There is only one happiness in life, to love and be loved.

Mignon McLaughlin – In the arithmetic of love, one plus one equals everything, and two minus one equals nothing.

Vincent van Gogh – There is the same difference in a person before and after he is in love, as there is in an unlighted lamp and one that is burning.

Jeanne Moreau – Age does not protect you from love, but love to some extent protects you from age.

Ralph Waldo Emerson – The only true gift is a portion of yourself.

Tipper Gore – When things get rough, you don't just cut and run.

Lisa Hoffman – Love is like *pi* – natural, irrational, and very important.

Luciano de Crescenzo – We are each of us angels with only one wing, and we can fly only by embracing each other.

André Maurois – A happy marriage is a long conversation which always seems too short.

Flora Davis – Actually a marriage in which no quarrelling at all takes place may well be one that is dead or dying from emotional under nourishment. If you care, you probably fight.

Joe Murray – Marriage should be a duet: when one sings, the other claps.

Ogden Nash
To keep your marriage brimming
With love in the loving cup,
Whenever you're wrong, admit it,
Whenever you're right, shut up.

SARCASTIC MARRIAGE QUOTES

And for those of you looking for something with a little more edge to it, you might want to refer to these quotations. Again, don't over do it, or you will lose the impact.

Clint Eastwood – There's only one way to have a happy marriage and as soon as I learn what it is I'll get married again.

Cullen Hightower – Courtship brings out the best. Marriage brings out the rest.

Lyndon B. Johnson – Only two things are necessary to keep one's wife happy. First, let her think she's having her own way. And second, let her have it.

Ann Landers – A successful marriage is not a gift; it is an achievement.

Dr Joyce Brothers – Marriage is not only a spiritual communion, it's also remembering to take out the trash.

Helen Rowland – Before marriage, a man declares that he would lay down his life to serve you; after marriage, he won't even lay down his newspaper to talk to you.

James Holt McGavran – There is a way of transferring funds that is even faster than electronic banking. It's called marriage.

Groucho Marx – Some people claim that marriage interferes with romance. There's no doubt about it. Anytime you have a romance, your wife is bound to interfere.

Mark Twain – Both marriage and death ought to be welcome: the one promises happiness, doubtless the other assures it.

Mae West – Marriage is a great institution, but I'm not ready for an institution yet.

Dick Martin – I belong to Bridegrooms Anonymous. Whenever I feel like getting married, they send over a lady in a housecoat and hair curlers to burn my toast for me.

Nancy Astor – I married beneath me. All women do.

Cher – The trouble with some women is they get all excited over nothing – and then they marry him!

Jean Kerr – Marrying a man is like buying something you've been admiring for a long time in a shop window. You may love it when you get it home, but it doesn't always go with everything in the house.

Johann Wolfgang von Goethe – Love is an ideal thing, marriage a real thing; a confusion of the real with the ideal never goes unpunished.

Socrates – By all means marry. If you get a good wife, you'll be happy. If you get a bad one, you'll become a philosopher . . . and that is a good thing for any man.

Mae West – Don't marry a man to reform him – that's what reform schools are for.

Tallulah Bankhead – No man worth his salt, no man of spirit and spine, no man for whom I could have any respect, could rejoice in the identification of Tallulah's husband. It's tough enough to be bogged down in a legend. It would be even tougher to marry one.

Zsa Zsa Gabor – A man in love is incomplete until he is married. Then he is finished.

I think you will agree that many of the quotes above are just wonderful. Any of them could work well as part of a wedding speech. Use them with care, and always give credit when due.

And when used well and sparingly, they will not only add that extra bit of star quality to your speech, but will help you to express your true feelings. Indeed, many of these quotes will inspire, motivate and encourage you, and help you to come up with powerful and emotive words of your own.

(16)

A Final Toast!

Whilst researching for this book, I discovered that, after they had got over the shock of realising they were going to have to make a speech, there were three key things that people making speeches at weddings were really concerned about:

1. Precisely what they were going to say, other than the formal stuff, and how they were going to find good material.

2. Finding the time to sit down and actually create the speech.

3. Dealing with their nerves on the day.

That's all.

I hope that by now, we have addressed all these plus a few more. But if I were to distil this book into a few short words and paragraphs, they would be these.

REMEMBER THE 5Cs

My key tests for a great wedding speech (or any other speech or presentation for that matter) are:

1. Clarity

Keep it simple and orderly. Don't clutter it with too much information. Speak carefully, thinking about what you are saying and listening to yourself.

2. Confidence

Rehearse what you are going to say – several times. Be familiar with your stories and anecdotes, and make a conscious effort to enjoy yourself. Remember that the nerves you feel are actually helping you to perform at your best.

3. Conviction

Be sincere about what you are saying and have respect for the people you are talking about. Be passionate about them and look people in the eye as you speak.

4. Connection

Make the effort to speak to as many of the guests as possible in person before you start your speech. When you come to make your speech, look people in the eye and smile. Even if you are using a microphone, remember to speak to *everyone* in the room or marquee or wherever the reception is being held. Don't forget the people at the back or they will feel left out.

If you are addressing remarks to the bride and groom, remember to turn to them as you speak – but don't make the mistake that so many speakers do, especially dads, of forgetting to face the guests.

5. Compassion

Show kindness and consideration for both the people you are talking about and the guests. Compassion is a great way of connecting with the guests – show genuine appreciation that they have attended, express real thanks for their gifts, cards and for giving up their time to come.

If you are the best man – don't overdo the humiliation of the groom!

ANYTHING ELSE?

Prepare it

First, take your speech seriously and put some effort into it. Most of us wouldn't dream of not preparing properly before a presentation to clients or the board (you don't?!), so it's surprising how few people do not put more effort into their wedding speech – which is infinitely more important than work. Too often, preparation of the speech is left to the last minute, and most of the so-called funny stuff is borrowed from other people. Don't do it – it doesn't work.

Start preparing your speech at least one month before the big day – ideally two. Spend the first week writing down notes of all your favourite memories and stories of family, friends, your fiancée, daughter, best man or the groom. Focus on telling these memories as stories or anecdotes. If they happen to be humorous, then so much the better, but don't focus on trying to have just humorous stories. Contrary to opinion, it's not compulsory to tell funny stories or jokes in your wedding speech. An unfunny story told well, will be more effective than a funny story told badly – every time.

Enjoy it

On the day, set out to enjoy yourself. Have a good time, and make your speech an integral part of your celebrations. It's a moment you want to remember. Of course you will be a bit nervous, but make a conscious point of remembering that *the nerves are helping you* to perform at your very best. If necessary, write this down on a piece of paper or on the back of a business card and keep it with you on the day. Refer to it just before your speech and smile!

Rehearse it

What will help you to really enjoy your speech will be the knowledge that you know what you are going to say, and have confidence in it. This means rehearsing several times! If you focus on telling stories as I have described above, you will find that you positively exude confidence, because stories are easy to recall. Remember, we tell stories all the time and everywhere we go – whether in the pub, the office, restaurants, the supermarket, the betting shop or on the bus. In particular, we tell stories with relatives and we are all very good at it.

Pace it

The secret of a really good speech is that it is remembered as part of the overall celebrations of the day, rather than being remembered in its own right. This may sound like exactly the opposite to what you would expect of a great speech, but the problem is that too many speeches are remembered for the wrong reasons. A good speech should be entertaining, but sincere, and should seamlessly flow through the celebrations of the reception. It should not come as an unwelcome interruption and, indeed, I have witnessed dozens of speeches that have done just that!

One moment the day had been progressing at an enjoyable and pleasant pace, with family and friends laughing, joking and enjoying themselves, only to come to a juddering halt after the speeches. Time and time again, I have seen the flow of the day brought to a complete standstill, leaving people wondering what to talk about in the silence immediately after the last speech. Often, this can be a cue for some people to decide to go home.

Just like a good host at a party knows when to top up drinks, the right time to serve dinner, the right time to turn up the music, the right time for an amusing story, the key is to keep everything moving along smoothly and we all know that there is an art to it. But the moment someone tells the wrong sort of joke, or brings up politics or fox hunting, you know it's all over. The atmosphere changes and all you want to do is be somewhere else. The same goes for wedding speeches – they must maintain or enhance the flow of the day.

Mean it

Many wedding speeches come over as slightly false, as though *too much* effort has been put in to making it memorable, when in fact quite the opposite has happened. This is usually the case when the groom, best man or father of the bride have left the planning and preparation too late and resorted to the internet or a joke book in an attempt to come up with something memorable.

Creativity in your speech is also fine, but again, don't go over the top. It can be embarrassing for the guests if it doesn't quite work. The British are particularly sensitive to this.

We discovered earlier in this book how many best men, fathers of the bride and grooms have a secret desire to kick off their career as a stand up comedian. I suspect it is something they have always wanted to do, and would, if they were brave enough, include a quick routine during presentations to colleagues and customers at work. Indeed, on one occasion I enjoyed an excellent presentation on '*How to Use Discretionary Trusts to Mitigate Inheritance Tax*' by someone who clearly had his place booked on the stage of the London Palladium. But most closet comedians in the office or factory save their 'best' work until the pub – or their wedding speech.

Equally, I have never understood why so many other people feel the need to burst into song at the slightest opportunity. I recently saw a motivational speaker at a business event, segue nicely between the importance of 'embracing change' to singing 'My Way' by Frank Sinatra.

I have also heard about a wedding where the groom started his speech with the usual welcomes and so on, and then with a flourish, produced an acoustic guitar from under the table to serenade his new bride – the best man's idea some 24 hours earlier. Apparently, it seemed like a good idea at the time.

The groom's choice of 'Green Eyes' by Coldplay was inspired, and he even changed the words to 'blue' eyes for the benefit of his wife. It was, as they say, 'their song' and the guests articulated their delight with a collective 'Aah'. It was just a shame that halfway through, he forgot the words.

Fortunately for our friend, his blue-eyed wife came dramatically to the rescue, leaping compassionately to her feet in an unselfish act of marital support and joined in the verse. For many of the guests, this moment had even more poignancy than the earlier marriage ceremony. Tears welled and mascara ran as the union of man and woman was consummated in song.

Coldplay themselves would have been taken aback by the cheer that erupted. 'More, more' came the cries as the guests now leaped to their own feet. Eventually, the cheers died down, and all that remained were the rosy pink blushes of the very happy couple. The groom lit a post-speech cigarette and puffed.

What can you say? An appalling moment was turned into something wonderful.

Sometimes, just sometimes, the wedding speech rules are there to be broken!

Postscript

I'm collecting wedding speech horrors. If you have a story of a wedding speech that went terribly wrong or was outstandingly good, please tell me about it. Simply send an email to enquiries@greatweddingspeech.com.

We may include some of them in the next edition of this book.

Resources

SPEECH PLANNING
Mind maps
Andrew Wilcox Consultancy
www.ajwilcox.co.uk

Illumine Limited
www.illumine.co.uk

Eric Sutherland
www.neuralpathways.org.uk

Shilpa Panchmatia
www.HumanXpression.co.uk

STORYTELLING
Doug Stevenson – Story Theater
www.dougstevenson.com

Marie Mosely
www.mariemosely.com

MAGAZINES
Stag and Groom
www.stagandgroom.com

SPEAKING AND PRESENTATION SKILLS

Professional Speakers Association
www.professionalspeakers.org

Training Strategies Limited
www.trainingstrategies.co.uk

Crystal Business Speakers Limited
www.crystalbusinessspeakers.com

Crystal Business Training Limited
www.CrystalBusinessTraining.com

PHOTOGRAPHY

David Calvert
www.calvert.biz
www.powerportraits.co.uk

Richard Trestain
www.imageandnature.com

MASTERS OF CEREMONIES AND TOASTMASTERS

www.londontoastmaster.com
www.toastmasternet.co.uk
www.thetoastmaster.me.uk
www.dwtoastmaster.com

TELEGRAMS

www.telegramsonline.co.uk

WEDDING SERVICES

Wedding Daze at Ecademy
www.ecademy.com
Search 'Wedding Daze'

PHILIP CALVERT'S PERSONAL NETWORK

For more tips, help and advice visit
www.ecademy.com
Search 'Philip Calvert'

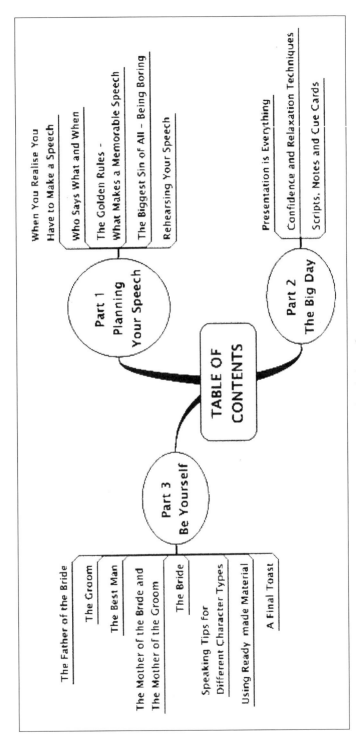

Sample mind map®.

Index